WHEN GOOD MEN ARE TEMPTED

Also by Bill Perkins

Awaken the Leader Within

When Young Men Are Tempted
(Bill Perkins and Randy Southern)

Six Battles Every Man Must Win

6 Rules Every Man Must Break

WHEN GOOD MEN ARE TEMPTED

UPDATED EDITION

BILL PERKINS

ZONDERVAN.com/
AUTHORTRACKER
follow your favorite authors

When Good Men Are Tempted
Copyright © 1997, 2007 by Bill Perkins

Requests for information should be addressed to:
Zondervan, *Grand Rapids, Michigan 49530*

Library of Congress Cataloging-in-Publication Data

Perkins, Bill, 1949 -
 When good men are tempted / Bill Perkins. — Updated ed.
  p. cm.
 Includes bibliographical references.
 ISBN-13: 978-0-310-27434-6
 ISBN-10: 0-310-27434-6
 1. Husbands — Sexual behavior. 2. Husbands — Religious life. 3. Lust —
Religious aspects — Christianity. 4. Sex — Religious aspects — Christianity.
5. Sex in marriage. 6. Sex instruction for men. I. Title.
 HQ28.P47 2007
 241'.66081 — dc22   2007013732

Published in association with the literary agency of Wolgemuth & Associates, Inc.

All Scripture quotations, unless otherwise indicated, are taken from the *Holy Bible, New Living Translation,* copyright © 1996. Used by permission of Tyndale House Publishers, Inc., Wheaton, IL 60189. All rights reserved.

Internet addresses (websites, blogs, etc.) and telephone numbers printed in this book are offered as a resource to you. These are not intended in any way to be or imply an endorsement on the part of Zondervan, nor do we vouch for the content of these sites and numbers for the life of this book.

Interior design by Beth Shagene

Printed in the United States of America

07 08 09 10 11 12 13 • 22 21 20 19 18 17 16 15 14 13 12 11 10 9 8 7 6 5 4 3 2 1

QG 11-13-15

*To Paul Saunders
and Phil Shaffer*

You're good men and good friends.

Contents

Introduction:
A Case of Identity Theft

About five years ago a friend of mine, Dr. Justin O'Brien, sat in my office and told me one of the most unsettling stories I'd ever heard.

"John Jones is an evil man," he said. "But when I first met him I thought he was an angel who would help my wife, also a surgeon, and me get the resources we needed to find a cure for AIDS."

"AIDS?"

"That's right," he said. "There's a lot of political stuff going on behind the scenes. Stuff the public knows nothing about. But I believed, and still believe, that a scientist I knew was close to a cure. He needed money and recruited me to help him get it."

"And that's where Jones enters the story?" I asked.

"Right. He captured my interest by describing the wealth of his family. He also mentioned personal friends — I'm talking about internationally famous people. He assured me they would be interested in donating to the cause."

"Weren't you suspicious?" I asked.

"Of course," he said. "That's why I hired a former FBI agent to do a background check."

"And ...?"

"He said the guy was squeaky clean and extraordinarily rich."

"So what happened?"

"He scammed me. And when he was done, my wife and I had lost our homes, cars, yacht, credit rating, savings, and investments. Bill, I didn't even have the money to buy a loaf of bread."

"So what's going on now?" I asked.

"He's about to be sentenced, and I had hoped you'd go to the hearing with me."

On March 23, 2002, John Robert Jones, alias George Robert Jones, was sentenced to ten years in the federal penitentiary for numerous crimes — including possession of a deadly weapon, interstate mail fraud, financial fraud, theft, and grand larceny. John Robert Jones stole my friend Dr. Justin O'Brien's identity and almost everything he owned.

As I watched him shuffle out of the courtroom, his legs linked together by chains, Jones turned in our direction and smiled. "I'll see you in hell," he shouted across the courtroom to my friend. "I'll get out. You watch. I'll get out."

As a cold chill raced down my back, my friend turned to me and said, "He'll keep his promise too. Just watch. And even if he doesn't, he'll continue to steal from other unsuspecting people from behind prison walls. All he needs is a computer."

I can't help but think how much Jones looked like any other man. Yet he had so thoroughly deceived my friend that it took Dr. O'Brien years to restore his identity as well as his lost wealth.

Often when a man falls into a sexual sin he thinks the core issue is about behavior. He tells himself, *If I could just stop flirting with women or surfing the Web, I'd be okay.*

There's a sense in which the problem *is* one of behavior, but that's not the core issue. The root issue is identity theft.

When a man trusts Christ as his Savior, God makes him a new man, a good man, in Christ. The identity a man is given is so new that it inspired the apostle Paul to write, "Therefore, if anyone is in Christ, he is a new creation; the old has gone, the new has come!" (2 Corinthians 5:17 NIV). This change is more radical than that which transforms a caterpillar into a butterfly. We who know Christ are, by nature, children of God.

Yet even though we're new men in Christ, we still must deal with the lustful appetites that reside within us. These have not been taken away or changed. But they do not define who we are. The problem is that for much of our lives those appetites exercised free access to our minds, exercising control over our thoughts and actions, and during that season of our lives our identity was defined by those evil thoughts and actions. We saw ourselves as lustful men who delighted in indulging our sexual appetites in any way we wanted — or at least we enjoyed fantasizing about such behavior.

If as new men we allow those same lustful desires to exercise control over our minds, we'll once more see ourselves, not as new men in Christ, but men driven by and controlled by our sexual appetites. In a sense, our sinful lust will have stolen our identity.

Such thinking and behavior is out of character with our new identity. In Christ you're truly a new and good man. But good men are tempted — and it's crucial for you to know how to respond when you face temptation.

This book isn't based on the belief that if you just think the right thoughts and look in the right places you'll live a pure life. It's based on the idea that as you understand who you are in Christ, you'll no longer let lust steal your identity and control your behavior. Indeed, as you comprehend your new and true identity, God will give you the power to live in a way that expresses your true self.

This concept is so radical, so revolutionary, so life changing, that if it grabs hold of your mind and spirit, you'll never be the same. You're about to embark on a journey that will forever free you from identity theft of the worst kind and release you to live like a son of God.

PART ONE

THE STRUGGLE

Why Naked Dogs Look So Dressed

This book was birthed one sultry Friday night in south Texas while I was turning on my sprinkler system. Because of an extended drought the city only allowed grass watering between midnight and six a.m. No big deal to me since I was a night owl.

As I walked across my backyard, I noticed my neighbors' lights were on. Curious as to why they were up so late, I approached the fence and looked through the slats. I expected to see a handful of people playing cards inside their home. Or at least, I convinced myself that's what I expected so see. Instead I saw a hot young brunette talking on the phone. That wouldn't have been any big deal if she had been dressed. But she wasn't.

Instantly my eyes locked on her. Adrenaline raced through my body.

In that moment my mind flashed back to the night I was playing on the swing set in the backyard of the home where I grew up in Roswell, New Mexico. As I swung up and down, to my right, I saw my older sister's bedroom light turn on. A moment later one of her high school friends, with the body of a goddess, undressed in front of the window. At the time I couldn't believe my good luck.

Yet on that balmy night in Texas I wasn't a kid. I was a thirty-year-old pastor, with a gorgeous wife, a son ... and ... and ... and I wondered, *What am I doing?*

After gazing at her for a few seconds, I pried myself away from the fence. Okay, it might have been more than a few seconds. But it wasn't a minute ... definitely not a minute. Anyway, as I walked away I felt intoxicated by the spectacular beauty of that naked woman's body. And I couldn't help but wonder why the form of a nude female would affect me that way.

Since that experience, I've addressed thousands of men around the world and talked personally with hundreds more. I've administered confidential surveys to find out what men are thinking and doing. In the process, I've discovered a reality that will no doubt surprise you as much as the presence of salt in the sea — namely, every man, Christian or otherwise, has his own personal battle with lust.

Those who disclaim such a battle are either in denial or lying. I guess they could also be dying and just too sick to think about sex. But even dying men may have sex on their mind. My eighty-seven-year-old father was talking about sex just hours before dying of pneumonia.

The point is, if you're a man you're wired to enjoy the beauty of a woman, and that enjoyment can take your mind and body to some sinful places with severe consequences. And I suspect you're reading this book because you're trapped in a sinful place and want out or you want a map to keep you from going there. Before providing you with such help, I want to talk about the question raised on the night I saw that *au naturel* brunette. Namely: why do naked women look so good?

Actually, I wrote this chapter and the next one after finishing the rest of the book. As I basked in the belief that I had banged out the last line of the last paragraph, a thought occurred to me. The more I contemplated this thought the more it bothered me. The thought flowed from my observing that a lot of Christian men, maybe even you, think it's sinful to enjoy looking at a beautiful woman.

Such thinking is reinforced by writers and Christian experts who, in an attempt to call men to sexual purity, decry not only adultery and pornography-fueled masturbation, but the act of drawing pleasure from a woman's beauty as well.

I just finished reading a popular book written to help Christian men live sexually pure lives. While the book provides helpful insights and practical suggestions, the author gives the impression that whenever a man derives pleasure from looking at a woman — he seemed to mean any woman in any situation — other than his wife, he has committed adultery, or at least foreplay, in his heart. In essence, he seems to insist that the magnetism a man feels for a beautiful woman who is not his wife is always fueled by and feeds sexual lust. So the author coaches the men to never look at a woman except his wife. With such superspiritual and utterly impossible standards, is it any wonder so many Christian men live under a load of failure and guilt?

I'm convinced your ability to enjoy the beauty of a woman is a gift from God. That doesn't mean God would approve of your feasting your eyes on Internet porn or the gyrating hips of the skimpily dressed girls who dance during a beer commercial. Nor is it okay for you to check out the lingerie ads in the morning paper — an entry point ritual for me. But I don't buy into the idea that if you're walking through a park and a gorgeous girl walks by it's wrong for you to notice her beauty and enjoy it. Would it be okay for you to ogle her? Or to follow her so you could continue "enjoying" her beauty?

Umm ... do you need me to answer that question? Come on ... you know the difference between glancing at a gorgeous girl and locking in your visual video recorder and capturing her every move for future reference. The key issue is for you to enjoy a woman's beauty without compromising your character and using her excellence to feed your lust.

"Okay," you may be asking, "how do I accomplish that?"

I'm convinced the first step down the path of sexual purity involves understanding why naked dogs look so dressed and — more importantly — why naked women look so good. Once we understand the sacred gift God has given us, we'll realize why we should cherish it and keep it pure.

I'd like to lift the magnetism you feel
toward beautiful women to the high and holy place
I believe God intended it to occupy.

The Mystery of a Woman's Beauty

When I saw my wife's body for the first time, I beheld something heavenly. Nothing in all of creation compared with the beauty of her nakedness. Being the modest type, she refused to run, or even walk, around our apartment naked ... even though I pleaded with her. I simply couldn't see enough of her unexcelled naked beauty. I remember feeling as though I shouldn't stare. But I wanted to stare.

Evolutionists strip the mystery from a woman's beauty. They tell us men are attracted to naked women because of natural selection. They reason that if men didn't find women attractive, they wouldn't be inclined to reproduce. While that makes sense, it also reduces sexual magnetism to a purely biological, animalistic experience. It isn't. God created men with sexual appetites. He wired us to be attracted to women.

There's more here than some sort of accidental evolutionary programming. The book of Proverbs addresses the magnetism between a man and a woman. Agur, son of Jakeh (some of those ancient Jews had weird names), described four things too amazing for him to understand. One of them was how a man loves a woman (Proverbs 30:19). That ancient sage couldn't decipher the mystery of the magnetism between a he and a she.

So why do naked women look so good? The answer may disappoint you like the punch line to a very long and bad joke. You see, there's something about the buzz men get when they look at a beautiful woman that defies understanding.

At the deepest level, nobody understands
the attraction between men and women.

It's kind of like sleep. Did you know that nobody fully understands why people need to sleep?[1] Doesn't that seem odd to you? Researchers understand what happens when we sleep and what occurs when we're sleep deprived. They can even state the benefits of sleep. But nobody knows exactly why humans need to sleep.

Similarly, we don't know why naked women look so good to men. God has created something wonderful for you that defies understanding. If, as though it were a mathematical formula, you could understand the attraction you feel for the female face and form, there would be no mystery.

So if someone ever asks you, "Why do naked women look so good?" you can answer, "Metaphysically, we just don't know." That will definitely impress them.

Having said that, there are aspects of the answer that are as simple as 2 + 2 = 4. For instance, naked women are beautiful because we seldom see them that way. This whole idea of nakedness is a special treat God has given only to people Animals, for instance, can't be naked.

Why Do Naked Dogs Look So Dressed?

Over the years I've had several dogs. My most recent was a 185-pound Great Dane. When I'd take him for a walk people would comment on his size and then ask me his name.

"He's Big," I'd say.

"He sure is," they'd reply. "What's his name?"

"He really is Big," I'd say as I patted his massive black head with my right hand.

Frustrated, they'd ask again about his name.

By then I was laughing as I explained, "That's his name, *Big*."

I gave him that name because I anticipated just such conversations. They always reminded me of the Bud Abbott and Lou Costello routine, "Who's on First?"

It's amazing how quickly I bonded with that Great Dane. If you have a dog, you understand how they blend into a family. They ride in our cars. They sleep with us (forget that one with Big). We talk to them as though they could understand us. Occasionally my boys even dressed Big in clothes. They'd slip red Nike shorts over his hind legs and a white sweatshirt over his front legs. Next they'd secure a hat to his head and sunglasses on his nose.

While Big looked cute all dressed up — umm, maybe stupid would better describe him — the truth is he didn't need shorts and a sweatshirt. Why? Because even without them he wasn't naked. No animal is ever regarded as naked. Think about it for a moment. Have you ever seen a dog strolling down the street without shorts and a shirt and wondered why it wasn't dressed? Of course not! And no cop ever ticketed a dog for indecent exposure.

Nothing can be naked in the same sense people are naked. Not trees, rocks, dogs, or dolphins. As men, we're not curious about the nakedness of an animal or plant. How could we be? They can't be naked. What man ever searched the Internet for pictures of naked dogs? (If you know, please don't tell me.) Women can be naked. Yet they seldom are. The women we see every day at work and in our communities are all clothed. A naked woman reveals what is almost always hidden from male eyes — the beauty of her body.

Comedian and television personality Tim Allen said he'll never forget the first time he saw a picture of a naked woman. He said, "In a way, the picture was both frightening and reassuring. I realized for the first time that, dumb as it sounds, all women are naked under their clothes.... That discovery made me distrust all women forever: they're hiding this! They have this power and I didn't even know it. It's just under their clothes!"[2]

Allen raises an issue that most men can identify with; namely, how can women walk around every day and hide something so wonderful? And how can they pretend they don't know what they're doing?

I find his comments amusing and helpful. Amusing because they so openly express what many men feel but would never say — at least, they wouldn't put it in writing. Helpful because they reveal part of the reason why naked women look so good: men want to see something beautiful that's been hidden from them.

The opening pages of the Bible give us additional insight into the mystery of a woman's appeal. In the next chapter we'll examine why God made naked women look so good.

FOR DISCUSSION

1. Can you remember the first time you saw a naked woman, either in person or in a photograph? How did it affect you? Can you still see the image in your mind? If so, what does that tell you?

2. How do evolutionists reduce sexual magnetism to a purely animalistic experience? What's the problem with such a view?

3. Proverbs 30:18–19 (NIV) says,

   There are three things that are too amazing for me,
   *   four that I do not understand:*
   *   the way of an eagle in the sky,*
   *   the way of a snake on a rock,*
   *   the way of a ship on the high seas,*
   *   and the way of a man with a maiden.*

   What do we learn about the attraction between a man and a woman from these verses?

4. How is nakedness unique to people? How does the fact that women are usually clothed affect men? Why?

5. How do you think most men believe God feels about the sexual attraction men have for women? What does that tell you about their view of God? Why do you think they view God that way?

Why Naked Women Look So Good

As I stand in a bookstore at Chicago's O'Hare Airport my eyes secretly caress the cover of the latest edition of a sports magazine that I seldom read. But the cover of this *Sports Illustrated* grabs my full attention. It shows the face and figure of the female who won the annual competition. I conspiratorially look around to make sure I don't know any of the other customers. Hopefully, none of them recognize me. I do not want anyone I know to see me peeking at *this* edition of *Sports Illustrated*.

As you've guessed I'm talking about the *Sports Illustrated Ugly-Dog Edition*. Every year that edition of the magazine outsells all others. Men not only buy it so they can salivate over the salacious image on the cover, but because they know the magazine is filled with pictures of other ugly dogs wearing dental floss thongs, lying sensually on a sandy Caribbean beach.

If only the images that wink at me from my television set and lure me from my computer monitor were dogs. As I noted in the last chapter, men don't search the Internet for images of naked dogs. No ... it's never a dog that summons me from a magazine cover in a bookstore. Why? Because advertisers know that dogs are good for selling dog food, dog leashes, and wireless fences. But an ugly-dog competition, or even a pretty-dog competition, won't sell copies of *Sports Illustrated*. Nothing attracts men to a magazine, the silver screen, or an office fax machine like the presence of a beautiful woman.

Some Christian guys hate this truth about themselves. Or think they should. Yet God designed women so you would find them attractive. Did you catch that? Please read the next sentence out loud: *God designed women so I would find them attractive.* That holy magnetism needs to be lifted to its rightful place. That involves understanding the six reasons why God made naked women look so good.

REASON ONE: To Replace Aloneness with Companionship

The moment I saw Cynthia Russell I melted. Like a bar of chocolate exposed to the sun I liquefied and spread out on my desk and dripped onto the floor. Somehow I managed to restore my premelted form. I sat at my desk with my heart pounding, hoping to get another glance of her flashing brown eyes.

At mealtime I wondered about her favorite food. At night I dreamed of her. When I walked to school I felt nervous at the thought of her. In class I never spoke a word to her. In young Cynthia's presence my jaw froze in place rendering my tongue as immovable as a ... well as immovable as an ice tongue. I did, however, carve a heart into my desk with an arrow going through it and the script: R + C (I used to go by my middle name, Randy for Randolph).

From the moment I first saw that angelic-faced girl in the first grade I knew my life would be incomplete until I married her. Of course, our union was not to be. But from that time on I felt a hole in my heart that only the girl of my dreams would one day fill.

Adam had no such experience to show him he needed a companion. He lived unaware of his aloneness because he didn't grow up surrounded by cute little girls. He didn't go to a high school or college where most guys had girlfriends. Since he was unacquainted with female companionship he could neither write nor appreciate the agony of a lonely heart as expressed in country western music.

Anyway, after each creative day, God looked at what he had made and announced: "It's good." Following the sixth and final day, during which he made Adam, God declared that his work was "very good" (Genesis 1:31).

But when God saw that Adam was alone, he said it was "not good" (Genesis 2:18). The Lord then determined to make a helper suitable for, or corresponding to, Adam — a helper who would complete him.

Before God did this, Adam needed to realize his need. To accomplish that, God had him name all the animals. Day after day, month after month, the animals — male and female — paraded before Adam, and he named them. Eventually, he realized no creature corresponded to him. Once Adam comprehended the "not good" state of being alone, God stepped in. He caused Adam to fall into a deep sleep and performed the first act of surgery. He took a rib from Adam's side and custom-made a companion for him.

God made sure her eyes, lips, hair, breasts, legs, feet, arms, and hands would be just what Adam wanted and needed. Like liquid beauty filling a glass, she would empty his world of aloneness — an aloneness that even God's presence couldn't remove (now, that's a profound thought).

When God had put the final touch on his masterpiece, he nudged her in Adam's direction and quietly disappeared.

Meanwhile, Adam woke up, rubbed his eyes, climbed to his feet, and wandered through the garden searching for an un-named animal.

Suddenly she stood before him. After years without anyone to talk with (I'm talking about a human being here, not God), walk with, laugh with, dream with, hold, or make love with, Adam beheld the crown of God's creation. Every woman since would pale before her perfection. She was flawless physically, spiritually, emotionally, psychologically, and intellectually. She possessed everything Adam needed in another person. And she carried no baggage from previous relationships. No corrosive bitterness. No ugly scars. No crippling regrets. No selfish expectations. No credit-card debt.

Does this give you insight into why you're attracted to beautiful women? They are the masterpiece of God's creation made to replace your aloneness with the perfect companion. But they're something else too. A woman fills up what you're lacking.

REASON TWO: To Complete You

To create Eve, God took a rib from Adam. When God brought Eve to Adam, he got back a new and much improved version of what he had lost. Without Eve, Adam was a red Porsche with no motor or a Learjet without fuel. He looked good on the outside but something was missing. When Adam met Eve, he came face to face, chest to breasts, thighs to thighs, with the part of himself that was missing.

While the Bible doesn't say this, I think the beauty of a woman's body is somehow linked to a man's search for com-pleteness. At the deepest level of a man's subconscious, is there a part of him that craves finding the one who will make him whole? Are we searching for the part that was taken from us? Are we seeking the one without whom we will forever feel incomplete?

I don't mean to imply that single people can't find fulfillment. After all, Jesus was single and his life was full. But most single people have learned to live with what is usually a mild case of aloneness, a sense that they are by themselves, that they are lacking something or someone — something or someone they've learned to live without.

I think that for men, that sense of aloneness or lacking is a figurative need to find their missing rib, a need to discover the person who will make them complete.

> *In the moment a man gazes*
> *at a woman's naked beauty,*
> *he experiences,*
> *for a fleeting second,*
> *the hope of being complete.*

God made naked women beautiful by creating them to complete us. How could we not feel magnetically pulled to one who has the power to fill up what's lacking in our life?

REASON THREE: So You Could Enter Her Glory

In his book *The Mystery of Marriage*, Mike Mason notes that the human body "possesses a glory that is unique in all the earth."[1] By glory he meant "awe-inspiring beauty." In a sense, our bodies reveal who we are. They're the physical expression of our soul and spirit. The body of a woman is more than skin and bones and blood and hair. It is the veil of her person. What a cool insight!

Several times in the Old Testament, we find God revealing himself with a physical manifestation. He did that when he first appeared to Moses on the mountain as a fire in a bush. Later he appeared to Moses and the Israelites at Mount Sinai as a dense cloud filled with lightning. The glory of God was so great at Mount Sinai that the face of Moses would literally glow after being in the presence of God's glory.

Theologians refer to these manifestations of God as his "shining glory." They reveal the power and beauty of God. I believe our physical bodies have their own shining glory. It's a beauty that in some small way reveals us as the masterpiece of God's creation.[2] As men, we never tire of looking at a woman's beauty. It's as if we want to view it from every angle and, like Moses on the mountain, enter her glory. Funny thing is, sometimes after a man has entered a woman's glory — his face also glows.

REASON FOUR: To Give You Intimacy

I don't know about you, but I haven't gotten naked around many women. While in college, before I met Cindy — who would later become my wife — I got naked with as many gorgeous coeds as I could. I look back with regret at that period of my life during which I had lost my spiritual ballast. But even without a growing friendship with Christ, nakedness was never a casual thing for me. If a girl took off her clothes in my presence, and I took off mine too, it wasn't because we were comparing tattoos.

The truth is, nakedness assumes intimacy. It assumes that the person who has disrobed in your presence trusts you. They're willing to let you see their beauty and their imperfections. We do that with people we believe will love and accept us — scars, warts, moles, flabby skin, wrinkles, skinny legs, balding head, and all.

Adam and Eve had such intimacy. After God brought them together, "The man and his wife were both naked, and they felt no shame" (Genesis 2:25 NIV). Their physical nakedness portrayed the nakedness that existed at a deeper level — a spiritual and emotional level. Adam and Eve were intimate in every sense of the word.

While men shy away from intimacy, they desperately need it. The problem is we've been programmed to believe real men are rugged, self-sufficient, and independent. While we grit our teeth and try to go it alone, inside we long for an intimate connection at the deepest level. I believe that naked women are beautiful because their nakedness tells us, "I'm here for you. I'm yours. I've bared myself for your eyes." That unspoken — or spoken — statement tells a man he's safe. It tells him he's loved. It tells him someone wants to be intimate with him.

One thing that bugs me about the gorgeous girls who parade their nude bodies before the invisible eyes of the Internet is that they give an illusion of intimacy. After I had spoken at a men's event one evening, a middle-aged man approached me and asked, "Bill, do you think it's okay for me to look at a naked girl on the Internet if I believe I may one day marry her?"

I looked at this guy and thought, *How could anyone be so idiotic?* I then said, "I can guarantee you not one of those girls you're looking at would give you the time of day. Their motivation is money and attention — not intimacy. And even if they would, God doesn't want your eyes looking on the beauty of a woman's naked body until she's your wife."

Yet because nakedness communicates a desire for intimacy these young women exercise a powerful attraction for men —

not just because of their curves, but because of the illusion of intimacy they offer (I'll talk about this later on).

> *Because nakedness presupposes intimacy,*
> *seeing a naked woman provides men with an intimate*
> *connection — even if it's a superficial one.*

God made naked women appealing to men by wiring us in such a way that we view nakedness as an offer of intimacy. True intimacy, however, can only occur in a safe setting, in an environment of love and trust.

REASON FIVE: To Provide a Sexual Playmate for You

Because Christians place a high value on sexual purity some people take that to mean God disapproves of sex ... all sex. That's why some people are surprised to learn that God didn't just create men and women as sexual creatures — he celebrates sex.

In fact, God didn't just design you so you'd enjoy playing with a woman's naked body, he created the ideal playground: marriage. Men and women who exchange marriage vows are making a commitment to pursue the intimacy that nakedness presupposes. It's only within marriage that a man can fully celebrate his wife's body.

Solomon certainly did. And he wasn't reluctant to express his pleasure. Tucked away in the middle of the Old Testament is the poetic book Song of Songs. The book describes the love between Solomon and his bride. The language is so sexually charged that for years theologians preferred to interpret the book allegorically rather than literally. By allowing Solomon to represent Christ and his young bride, the church, they could get around the sexual language. But such an interpretation doesn't do justice to the text or to God's high view of sexual intimacy.

A Garden That Pleases

In his book *A Song for Lovers*, my friend S. Craig Glickman said of the couple, "Their love is consummated in one of the shyest and most delicate of love scenes in world literature."[3] There's nothing crude or rash in Solomon's speech. Instead he compares his bride to a garden and fountain (vv. 12–15). He makes a gentle reference to her virginity by noting that the fountain is sealed and the garden locked (v. 12). Nobody else has entered her garden. Finally the night for a visitor has arrived. Solomon delights in the aroma and taste of her love.

In response to his expressions of delight, she invites him to come into her garden (v. 16). Before doing so, he finds himself swept away by her beauty and describes it more fully. Her garden is like a paradise of fruits, flowers, blossoms, trees, and aromatic spices.[4] As any man who has experienced sexual intimacy with a woman will attest, that most private of all places is, as Solomon noted, a garden of great pleasure.

Is she ready for his love? Indeed. Solomon declared that her fountain has become a "well of flowing water" (v. 15). Sexually aroused, she pleads with him to "come into his garden and taste its choice fruits" (v. 16). Hello! It doesn't take a professor of literature to explain the meaning of Solomon's language.

A Word of Approval

After allowing us to peek into his honeymoon suite, Solomon permits us to hear the final words that were uttered that night. Amazingly, they weren't spoken by Solomon or his bride. They were spoken by God. And how did the creator of a woman's beauty respond to the pleasure the couple enjoyed? He said, "Eat, O friends, and drink; drink your fill, O lovers" (Song of Songs 5:1).

The One who created them man and woman gave hearty approval to their evening of sexual pleasure.

Reason Six: To Provide You with a Sexual Bridle

God intended the act of sexual intercourse to be among the most powerful and pleasurable experiences of life. In the joining together of a man and a woman, the two become "one flesh." Their bodies are literally linked together. During those exhilarating moments, the man and woman are whole again. They are one. And it feels good too.

God's ideal is for this oneness to take place within the safety of marriage. From the beginning God's ideal was for one man to remain with one woman throughout life (Genesis 2:24). While God made naked women beautiful to men, he only wants a man to enjoy the nakedness of one woman — his wife.

Why? In part because the marriage bed provides us with a means of satisfying and controlling our sexual appetite. As fallen creatures, if not controlled, that powerful force could drive us to seek self-gratification in all the wrong places. No man should forget that he corrals a ravenous beast with an insatiable appetite. And while that beast may occasionally sleep, he will never stop wanting to run wild.

As a boy, growing up in Roswell, New Mexico, our family owned some quarter horses that we kept on ten acres outside of town. Early on, my dad acquainted me with a saddle and bridle. While the saddle helped me stay on a horse, the bridle enabled me to control an animal much larger and more powerful than me.

Marriage is like that bridle. Without it, our passions will run out of control — hurting us and others.

A Dropped Bridle

Of course, if our marriages are going to become the playground in which we enjoy a woman's nakedness, we must be attracted to our wife. Several years ago I was counseling a man who had been married five years. He took pride in his physical conditioning, appearance, and fast-track career.

As we sat across form one another at a coffee shop, he said, "I don't find Julie attractive anymore. She doesn't turn me on."

"Why are you talking to me, dude?" I asked. "You need to see an eye doctor. She's gorgeous." (I only use the "dude" word with special friends.)

"Ever since the birth of Justin, her breasts have sagged. I want her to get a boob job. Not a big one. You know, maybe a D cup."

"Seems big to me."

"Think so?"

"Look, Jason, it's just a matter of time until both your bodies show the signs of aging. If you get on the treadmill of plastic surgery, she'll end up with an endless series of facelifts, tummy-tucks, breast implants, and liposuction procedures."

"Yeah, we were thinking about going ahead with a tummy tuck while she was on the table. You know — fix that too."

"Jason," I said. "You're not getting it. Your reasoning is flawed."

"How so?" he asked — giving me permission to tell him what I would have said anyway.

"The magnetism of a magnet isn't based on the physical appearance of the magnet but on the makeup of the magnet. It's what's on the inside that pulls the opposite poles together."

Jason didn't care. His wife got her "boob job," and then he complained that her breasts didn't "feel" right. Listen, when a man and woman are no longer physically attracted to one another, it indicates that their relationship with God and each other is strained to the breaking point. Something on the inside needs attention.

Once a man turns his back on God, and his wife, his marital vows quickly lose their power. Instead of harnessing his passions and directing them toward his wife, he's allowing them to run wild. When that happens, he no longer treats his wife as his companion who completes him and provides him with intimacy. He stops thinking of her as his one and only God-given sexual playmate or as God's masterpiece whose body is the glory of her person.

Marriage is no longer a playground, but a prison from which he wants out. And his wife is an obstacle to his own sensual gratification, someone he must change to meet his needs or get away from so his needs can be met by another woman — or an image of a woman.

Such thinking opposes God's intention for men. He has commanded us to focus our sexual energies on satisfying our wife — not ourselves. (I'll talk about how to do this in chapter 18.) As men we must remember that our body is there for our wife — that means our eyes are to look upon her naked beauty and enjoy her beauty alone (1 Corinthians 7:3–5). We are never to allow our eyes to enjoy the beauty of a woman in a way that would demean our wife.

That's the ideal we must strive for. And the purpose of this book is to help good men, like you, who want to please God and live pure lives, develop a strategy for resisting sexual temptation. It's written to give you a workable plan, in God's power, to stay pure whether you're single or married. Then, and only then, will you experience the kind of intimacy and pleasure God intends you to find in the heart, and in the arms, of your wife.

What about Other Women?

Of course, there is a problem that stands in the way. While the ability to enjoy the beauty of a woman is a gift from God, it's also a gift that can be easily abused. If you're single you'll face the temptation to enjoy a woman's beauty sexually prior to marriage. And if you're married, even if you're married to a beautiful woman, there will be times when you'll find other women more attractive. Their appeal may be so strong it pulls you away from your wife. During such times you'll be tempted to look for sexual pleasure in the wrong place.

Now that we understand why naked women look so good (thank you, God, for this gift), in the next chapter we'll see why women we can't have — or shouldn't have — often look better than the one God has given us.

FOR DISCUSSION

1. How does God view the sexual pleasure a man finds in his wife? What does Song of Songs 5:1 tell us about this question?

   I have come into my garden, my sister, my bride;
   I have gathered my myrrh with my spice.
   I have eaten my honeycomb and my honey;
   I have drunk my wine and my milk.

   Eat, O friends, and drink;
   drink your fill, O lovers.

2. Why do men find women so attractive? List each of the reasons noted in this chapter — which one applies most specifically to you?

3. What purpose does marriage serve in regard to a man's sexual appetite? In what ways is marriage God's way of providing for and protecting a man?

4. As you think through these questions, ask God to help you view women and sex as he does.

Why Other Women Look Better

I tried to sneak back into the house without waking my wife. With slow fluid movements I opened and closed the sliding glass door. With the stealth of a cat burglar I tiptoed across the den and down the hall. I silently opened the bedroom door and floated like a vapor across the room and into the bed.

"What took so long?" Cindy asked.

"What took so long?" I asked — my mind racing for a reply.

"That's what I'm asking you," she said.

"Oh, you mean why did it take me so long to turn on the sprinkler system?"

Getting suspicious, she turned on her night-light and sat up. I think my rapid breathing, drum-sounding heartbeat, and high-pitched voice indicated something was up.

"I wasn't gone that long," I said. "Definitely less than a minute."

"Longer than that," she said. And then silence as she waited with the patience of a cat for a mouse, or in this case a rat, to exit his hole.

"Uh, let's see … I guess what took me so long was that I saw a naked woman." I whispered, hoping my gentle voice would soften the impact of my words.

"What do you mean, you saw a naked woman?" she asked in a curious and surprisingly nonjudgmental voice — although it was louder than mine.

"You know," I said. "I saw a naked woman while I was standing at the fence looking through our neighbor's window."

"What were you doing looking through our neighbor's window in the middle of the night?"

"I saw the light on in their house and wondered what they were doing," I said.

"Oh," she said as she turned off the light. "I hope it doesn't happen again."

While Cindy fell asleep I relived that voyeuristic experience in my mind. As my pulse rate jumped to around 250 BPM I realized how seeing that gorgeous brunette wearing only a telephone on her left ear turned me on. And my excitement scared me because I knew I'd be turning on the sprinkler system every night for most of the summer.

When I climbed out of bed the next morning I knew I'd either have to fess up to my band of brothers or keep the previous night's experience a secret. Every Saturday morning the four of us met to encourage and challenge each other as husbands, fathers, and followers of Christ.

These guys were spiritual leaders in the church, and I valued their friendship and respect.

The last thing I wanted to do was look bad in their eyes. Yet more than their rejection, I feared repeating my misdeed. So I decided telling them was the best chance I had of not checking up again on my neighbor's midnight card game.

After a few minutes of small talk, I cleared my throat. Feeling as insecure as a cow at a slaughterhouse I told my story. What happened next surprised me more than my response to the girl next door.

One of my friends shifted nervously in his chair. "I know how you feel," Joe said. "I've been watching my neighbors for almost two years! From the second floor of our house, I can look right into their bedroom."

Well, that made be feel better ... and worse. But the story's not over. No sooner had he finished talking than Dave, a guy with the demeanor of Clark Kent, said, "My neighbor's an attractive single woman. I discovered a few months ago that she cleans her house at night in the nude. Because our houses are close together, I can see her clearly. I've been occasionally turning off my lights and watching her for two months."*

"Occasionally?" I asked.

"Once every couple of weeks," he said.

"When your wife's not home?"

"That's not true," he said. "There were nights I snuck over to the window when she was in another room."

"You never invited her to check out your neighbor's cleaning uniform?"

"Maybe I should have," he said.

"Each time I'd look into their bedroom I'd feel dirty," Joe said. "I'd swear it would never happen again. And yet, I found myself repeatedly drawn to the window."

After listening to these guys I knew I was nostril deep in dung. If they couldn't walk away from the lure of an erotic window show, how could I? But the more we talked the more I knew how we could guard ourselves from future temptations to invade a neighbor's privacy. (I'll share the rest of the story later.)

---

*Since the publication of this book I've received emails questioning the truthfulness of this story. It's true, except for Joe's name. Dave and I are still close friends and accountability partners.

That meeting served as a wake-up call. As a thirty-year-old pastor, I lived with the illusion that devoted followers of Christ had their lust under control. Until the previous night, I had successfully guarded my heart and eyes. I just figured other guys had too. Yet two of the best guys in the church had a big-time problem — and I knew I was on the same path.

After my sexual lust roared out of the cage, I wanted to know as much as possible about sexual sins. I've spent years reading, researching, interviewing, talking with counselors — all in an effort to understand the reasons for sexually compulsive behavior — or as the Bible calls it: enslavement to sin. I figured the more I understood my problem, the better I could overcome it. This book is the result of my attempts to develop a biblical strategy for my own sexual purity and the men I've met with over the years. And it's a strategy for resisting temptation that works.

I'm convinced that to win the battle for purity, we need to understand why we men are attracted to women we can't or shouldn't have.

The Dark Side

You understand, don't you, that all men are fascinated by things that are off limits. Both our experience and the Bible prove this to be true.

When I was a boy, my mother repeatedly told me, "Don't eat candy before dinner."

What a joke. I didn't care if candy ruined my appetite for meatloaf. I preferred candy to any meal she would put on the table.

Once I found a copy of *Playboy* magazine. My parents tried to convince me I shouldn't look at pictures of naked women. And how did I respond? I told them I'd comply, but I never did. Why? Because the undressed women I saw in *Playboy* looked better than fully dressed women. Much better.

After I got married a single friend asked me what it was like being married. "You know," he said, "now that you can have sex as often as you want?"

"It's great," I said. "Why, I never even notice other women. It's like they don't exist."

"Really?" he said.

"No. I'm kidding. In some ways it's worse. Because I know that I can never ever be with another woman I'm more attracted to than her."

You can imagine how that reality went over the first time I introduced it to my wife. "So, you don't think I'm pretty?" she said.

"No, hon. I'm not saying that."

"You like looking at other women more than me?"

"I like looking at you," I said, "but ... well, you know how you like chocolate?"

"You're not getting out of this that easily," she said.

"No, I'm serious. When you decide you'll never eat chocolate again, doesn't that make you want it even more when you see a chewy chocolate in a bowl? It's not just me!" I assured her. "All men are that way."

Just the other day we talked about the same subject. "Look at Tom Cruise," I said. "You gotta admit Nicole Kidman is gorgeous. Yet he dumped her for Penelope Cruz and then later married Katie Holmes. And Brad Pitt dumped beautiful Jennifer Aniston for Angelina Jolie and who knows how long that will last. Every year there are new stories of famous men with gorgeous wives who dump them for someone else."

"Well, those guys aren't Christians," she said.

"Just because a guy's a Christian doesn't mean he suddenly isn't a man. And fallen men are flawed in such a way that they find themselves attracted to women they can't have."

In spite of this reality, I've repeatedly assured Cindy I'm capable of having her be the most appealing woman in my life. But keeping her in the number-one spot requires understanding and discipline: understanding of myself and why other women often look better, and discipline to make choices that focus my sexual energies on her.

Forbidden Sex Looks Better

In the previous chapter we saw that God wired men to delight in a woman's beauty. That's good! It's healthy and normal. But that appeal turns sinful when our appreciation for a woman's beauty taps into our lust and we no longer see her as a person but as a body to be used for our pleasure. The transition from admiration — which is a healthy male response — to lust follows a well-worn path started by Adam and Eve.

Something happened to those two that sheds light on the process from a harmless look to a sinful decision. To begin with, there was nothing inherently wrong with the forbidden fruit (Genesis 2:17). It wasn't poisonous or rotten. On the contrary, it was something good that God told Adam and Eve to avoid. Why? To test their willingness to serve him and to give them an opportunity to exercise their free will. God gave them the freedom to choose what they would do with their lives.

Sometimes wrong things are good things that are off-limits. Like narcotic drugs. Used medically they relieve pain. Used illegally they can lead to addiction and death. On other occasions wrong things are good things used to excess — like sex, alcohol, or food. Sex and the beauty of a naked woman are good gifts from God. But sex sours when it's used compulsively or addictively.

I think Adam and Eve wouldn't have given the forbidden fruit a second look if the Serpent hadn't deceived Eve into believing that instead of dying if she ate it, as God had promised, she would become like him (Genesis 3:1–5).

Once she swallowed the lie, the fruit would be next. The more she looked at it, the tastier it appeared. Even though Eve had everything she needed, Satan deceived her into believing she had needs God couldn't meet.

Do you think Satan has developed a new and updated strategy to trip you up sexually? Of course not. He hasn't changed his scheme over the centuries. Today he tricks us into believing the sexual experiences God has forbidden will satisfy better than his provision of a wife.

While a one-night stand, an affair, or masturbating in front of your computer monitor will bring pleasure, it won't last. Solomon said, "The lips of an adulteress drip honey, and her speech is smoother than oil; but in the end she is bitter as gall, sharp as a double-edged sword" (Proverbs 5:3–4 NIV).

Solomon didn't deny the beauty of the other woman. Nor did he diminish the sweet pleasure she offered. Adam and Eve probably enjoyed the taste of the forbidden fruit. But the sweet savor of sin morphed into mud while still in their mouths.

Behind the Scenes

We all know, at least on an intellectual level, that the pleasure of sin is momentary. But we're still vulnerable to the lie that tells us forbidden fruit will satisfy. We long to taste its sweetness. And we'll struggle with the temptation to experience taboo sex as long as we live.

Why are women who are clearly off-limits so attractive? I find part of the answer a bit spooky. You see, I'm convinced Satan has the power to give women (or anything else) we shouldn't have, an appeal that lures us to them like mosquitos to a bug zapper. He did that with Eve, and he does it with us. Behind the scenes, there's something spiritual going on.

The Dragon Within

While Satan can tempt us, ultimately he can't force us to make a bad decision. That's up to us. And when we choose to lust after forbidden beauty on the Internet or at work or through a neighbor's window, our decision is driven by our own selfish and evil appetites.

On my eighth birthday my parents gave me a BB gun. Its cold steel barrel and carved wooden stock made it a weapon of wonder. The gun and I formed a deadly partnership. Cans, bottles, road signs — nothing escaped our attack.

Well, almost nothing. One afternoon I raised my gun and aimed at a sparrow perched on a branch in the willow tree in our backyard. Just as I was about to squeeze the trigger, my older sister, Patsy, ran into the yard waving her arms and yelling. As the bird fluttered away, she looked at me and smiled. She said nothing, but her smug face taunted, "Ha! Ha! Ha! Ha! Ha! I showed you who's in charge."

In that moment something inside took control. I lowered the barrel and aimed at my sister. A look of horror replaced her smug confidence as she took off at a full run. I aimed at the part of her I considered most heavily padded and thought, "Sit on this!" as I pulled the trigger. The BB found its mark, and she grabbed her butt and yelped. She darted into the house screaming, "I've been shot! I've been shot!" For a brief moment I wondered what had made me do something so stupid — then I realized I enjoyed it. That's why I shot her. It felt good ... to me. Not her.

My pleasure was short lived as my dad quickly removed his belt and proved he was as good an aim with a belt as I had been with my BB gun. Patsy delighted in my pain and celebrated when Dad confiscated my prized possession. I never again laid eyes on my weapon of wonder. But while Dad had the power to take away the tool I used for evil, he wasn't able to remove the dark side of my personality that enjoyed doing wrong.

That's the other part of the problem, isn't it? It's not just that we've got a spiritual enemy who entices us to do wrong, a part of us enjoys sin. All of us have areas in our lives where, from time to time, we're bent toward sexual sins. Christian men know they should remain pure, but many of them end up looking too long at a skimpily dressed girl at the gym, surfing the Internet for erotic sites, visiting strip clubs, flirting with a coworker, or sleeping with their girlfriend.

We know what God wants from us, yet we disregard his will. The particulars of our inner battles differ, but we all struggle with duplicity.

> *A part of us enjoys stepping over*
> *the moral line and finding pleasure*
> *in forbidden sex.*

And we've all promised to reform. Haven't we? Whenever I have a Q&A about sexual purity with male college students someone will ask about masturbation. I tell them I've got a chapter in my book entitled, "Masturbation: How to Beat It."

After they give a hearty laugh I let them know the title is really: "Masturbation: Getting a Grip on a Hard Subject."[1]

Once the laughter dies down everyone agrees it's a difficult habit to break. Is there a Christian guy alive who hasn't promised God he would never again masturbate, or at least cut back on the frequency? Yet keeping that well-intentioned promise works about as well as a duck deciding not to quack.

My purpose here isn't to discuss the subject of masturbation (I'll do that later) but to point out the fact that all men have made promises to reform impure or compulsive sexual behavior and failed to maintain their commitment.

The Dragon Awakens

Okay, so we've seen that other women sometimes look better. We also learned that Satan and his evil army have the power to coat taboo sexual objects and experiences with a deceitful glitter that glows ... in a way that appeals to our sinful appetites like gold coins to a dragon.

Of course, the dragon of our sin may hibernate. That's what happened to me. While I had struggled with sexual lust before following Christ, once I devoted myself to him, the struggle became less severe. I don't mean it disappeared. It just wasn't something I thought about as an issue in my life.

And then that night I looked through a neighbor's window the dragon roared out of his cave, breathing fire from his nostrils and threatening to take over my life. When that happens, we realize we're not the master in our home — the dragon is — or soon could be.

As the apostle Paul observed his own behavior, he concluded, "It is no longer I myself who do it, but it is sin living in me" (Romans 7:17 NIV). When Paul referred to himself as "I," he spoke of his redeemed core personality, that part of him that sought after God. He spoke of that place in his personality where God's Spirit lived. He referred to his true inner self that had been recreated by God and was truly a good man in Christ.

It's crucial for you to understand that this new, good man, is your true identity. And while you're a new man, you're not free of temptation. Indeed, as a good man you'll face temptation daily.

Paul knew that his true self, the good man, the part of himself that was united with Christ, wasn't carrying out the wrong behavior. Instead it was his sinful propensity and its dragonlike appetites that had taken over his mind and enslaved his will. Paul wasn't justifying or minimizing his sinful behavior. Nor was he shifting responsibility away from himself. Instead he was stating a fact. The true Paul, the new man in Christ, the good man in Christ, the man who desired to do right, wasn't the one doing evil. Instead it was the dragon of his sinful lust that had gained dominion over him.

While I know Paul wasn't enslaved to sexual impurity, like everyone else he had the potential to be enslaved (Romans 7:14–20). Even though he kept his sin under control, it continually tried to dominate his new man. He knew that the dragon within had the power to make him a prisoner. In fact, he said he knew what it was like to be its prisoner (Romans 7:23).

About the Other Woman

Of course, we all understand that knowing what to do doesn't guarantee doing it. In the garden, Eve knew what God wanted from her. So did Satan. In fact, Satan used the commandment of God to tempt her. He asked Eve, "Did God really say ... ?"

(Genesis 3:1). That question regarding what God had forbidden was the starting place of her temptation.

Few things stir up our sinful appetites like the word *forbidden*. Once we hear the word we immediately exempt ourselves. For instance, what do you instinctively want to do when you're driving down an interstate and see a sign that says, "Speed Limit 55 mph"? Do you smile and say, "Oh, good. I like going slow. I'm glad the state has forbidden me from going faster than 55"? I sure don't. I want to disobey. I want to drive faster. After all, I reason, nobody cares as long as I don't go too much faster. And with that lucid line of reasoning, I've exempted myself from the law.

> *Nothing excites the dragon*
> *in our soul like a rule*
> *declaring something off-limits.*

That's how your sin uses the laws of God to gain dominion over your life. Here's how it works. You'll read the words of Jesus that say if you look lustfully at a woman you've committed adultery in your heart (Matthew 5:28). So you say to yourself: "I'll never look at a hot girl again. I'll never look at a hot girl again. I'll never look at a hot girl again."

Do you see what's going on? All this time you're reviewing what God wants you to do, or not do, you're thinking about the hot girl you won't look at again. Your statement that you'll obey God is a declaration of war between the good man in you, the new man in Christ, and the dragon — your sinful appetites. And if that's the extent of your battle plan, you'll lose every time. Knowing the right thing to do does not guarantee success.

No man in the ancient world had a better grasp of God's Law than King David. He was a man who had it all. He'd conquered his enemies and brought peace to Israel. He had a loving wife and close friends. Not only was he a military genius, but he was a poet as well. He penned many of the psalms as an expression of his love for God.

As a reward for his faithfulness, God promised David a kingdom that would endure (2 Samuel 7:16). If anybody knew the right thing to do, it was David. And he certainly knew he shouldn't sleep with Bathsheba, the wife of Uriah the Hittite, one of his mighty men. She was definitely forbidden fruit.

Yet at a time when he should have been with his troops in the battlefield, David was at home. Why? I think he stayed home because he had been checking out Bathsheba and wanted a chance to be alone with her. I suspect he had told himself time and again it would be wrong to gaze at her naked beauty. And even worse to sleep with her. Yet instead of looking after his army, one night he stood on the roof of his palace and watched Bathsheba bathe (2 Samuel 11:1–27). What a rush that must have been.

David's unseen enemy had done what Goliath couldn't. He had glamorized the beauty of a naked woman, and her loveliness surfaced the dragon in his soul. Like other men, David wanted the woman God said was off-limits. Why? Because his sinful appetites were aroused by the idea that he shouldn't or couldn't have her. And so are yours. The dragon within you wants one thing: total domination of your life (Romans 7:23). And it will use God's law to enslave you.

That's Taboo

As I've addressed men's groups across the country and talked privately with other men, I've concluded that many Christian guys believe they're fighting a losing battle with lust. And it's a battle they're ashamed to talk about. Why? Because in Christian circles, sexual sins are serious — as they should be. But that legitimate seriousness can also create a fear of misunderstanding or rejection, and that fear often drives men to isolation. In every sense of the word, sexual sin is a taboo topic among Christian men.

That reality intensifies the problem of lust. Pornography, prostitution, and affairs all give the illusion of intimacy. The best way to combat that illusion is with real intimacy, or openness, with another person. Since most men haven't got that friendship connection, the power of lust intensifies. Other women become irresistibly attractive because of the illusion of intimacy they provide.

The Bottom Line

"Okay," you may be asking, "what's the bottom line here?" Let me review and then draw a conclusion.

We know that God created a mystery — men find the body of a naked woman beautiful. But that mystery hides a danger because men also find women other than their wife attractive. In fact, it may be the women we can't have look better than the one we can. Why? Because:

- Evil spiritual forces glamorize them
- Our sinful appetites are attracted to anything that's off limits
- The law of God that commands us to flee immorality stirs up our lust
- The illusion of intimacy is often more compelling than reality

- We're isolated from other men and can't talk through our struggles

Hopefully, you now see why good men are tempted. They need a strategy to enable them to find victory one temptation at a time. It could be that the magnitude of your struggle may cause you to feel you're facing a losing battle. A number of years ago I heard a story that puts our battles with sexual temptation into perspective.

The Incurable Itch

Once upon a time, a young man moved into a cave in the mountains to study with a wise man. The student wanted to learn everything there was to know. The old sage supplied the student with stacks of books. Before departing, the wise man sprinkled an itching powder on the student's hands.

Every morning the wise man returned to the cave to monitor his student's progress. "Have you learned everything there is to know?" the wise man asked.

And every morning his student would answer, "Not yet."

The wise man then sprinkled the itching powder on his student's hands and left. Every day for months the sage repeated this scenario. One day as he entered the cave the student reached out, grabbed the bag of powder, and tossed it into the fire that warmed the cave.

"Congratulations," the wise man said with a smile. "You've graduated. You now know everything you need to know."

"How's that?" the student asked.

"You've learned that you don't have to wait until you've learned everything before you can do something positive," he replied. "And you've learned how to take control of your life and stop the itching."

It could be that your struggle with lust has created a relentless itch in your soul. You've scratched it, hoping it would get better. But it hasn't. Instead it demands more attention. You may have repeatedly promised yourself and God that you'd get your act together. But the itching persists, and you can't make it stop.

In a way, that's the aim of this book: to help you, the new you in Christ, the good man, take control of your life through the power of God's Spirit, and stop the itching. But the book's purpose goes beyond that. It seeks to help you become not just a man who can resist temptation. But to help you develop your identity in Christ so that the good man in you lives, not only a pure life that pleases God, but a life of joy created by the knowledge that your heart and passions belong to one woman.

The remainder of this book will help you understand the good man Christ has created within you so that your sexual thoughts and actions will flow from him rather than your lust.

FOR DISCUSSION

1. What role do evil spiritual forces have in a man's attraction to other women?

2. Have there been times when you deceived yourself into believing you could enjoy sex outside of marriage and get away with it? What line of reasoning led to this distorted thinking?

3. What's the difference between appreciating a woman's beauty and lusting after her?

4. How does the previous story about the man with the itch give you hope?

5. What do you want to get out of this book? How does your answer compare with the last two paragraphs of this chapter?

The Power of
Taboo-Charged Sex

"What a bummer," I said as I slapped the *Oregonian*, Portland's major newspaper, and then tossed it onto the kitchen counter.

A few hours later while sipping a double espresso at Ricardo's, a local Italian restaurant, a friend joined me. After the waiter took our order and brought him a latte, my friend asked, "Did you hear about the fire at Adult Fantasy Video?"

"I just read about it this morning. I'm glad it's gone but ..."

"I feel sorry for the guy who died," Josh said before I could finish. "He was my age. He visited the place for a little fun and got trapped in a room with a raging fire between him and the front door."

"And no rear exit," I said.

"Imagine his terror when he ran down that narrow hall toward the back of the smoke-filled building and hit a brick wall," Josh said.

"You know who I feel sorry for?" I asked.

"Who?"

"His mother. She told the reporter he had probably only visited the place a few times."

"Wishful thinking," Josh said.

"It's irrelevant," I said angrily — not at Josh but at the stupidity of the guy who burned up. "Now that he's dead, does it matter? Her last memory of him will be where and how he died. She'll remember her baby boy as a pile of ashes on the floor of a sleazy porn shop."

"It could have been me," Josh said.

Confused by his comment, I stared at him for a few seconds. "What do you mean?"

"I've been in that place … the room where he died. Bill, you could have been reading about me in the paper this morning. You could be feeling sorry for my mom and wife and kids."

"I guess you got lucky. Will you go back?" I asked.

"I can't," he said. "It burned to the ground."

He's right. But that's not the end of the story. The city slapped the owner's hand for a fire-code violation, and his insurance company gave him a big enough settlement to rebuild the store. Now it's bigger and better than ever.

And what about Josh? A few months after the store reopened, I asked if he had visited it.

"I've been there," he said.

"Why?"

"I don't know. I guess I wanted to make sure the place had a back fire exit. You know, looking out for the other customers."

"Right."

"Bill, I hate that place. Every time I leave, I feel like I've swum through a sewer. I promise God I'll never return. And then a few weeks later I'll drive by, see the sign, and I can't resist the urge."

His words remind me of my two friends in Texas and other guys I've known over the years who are hooked on the taboo images of Internet porn or the forbidden girls in strip clubs or the rush of an office affair.

It's simple to step into the trap of sexual lust. Getting out is another matter. The jaws of the trap are steel strong and its teeth razor sharp. The good news is you can get free and avoid getting caught in the future. But it probably won't happen without an understanding of how the trap works. That's why in this chapter we'll examine the nature of sexual compulsions, why they're so powerful and the cycle of temptation we need to break.

Taboo-Charged Lust

Wouldn't it be great if once a man chooses to follow Christ his sexual lust was zapped with a spiritual laser? Occasionally a guy will approach me at an event where I'm speaking and say, "I thought once I got right with God my struggles with sin would be over. I think they've gotten worse."

Of course, one reason that's true is because before becoming a Christian many guys never resisted their sexual urges so there was no struggle. Once they became a Christ follower they entered an internal battle to harness those desires.

> *Unfortunately, many churches create an environment where sexually compulsive behavior thrives.*

Why? Because secrecy and risk increase the adrenaline rush associated with sexual sins. In a sense, they act like a turbocharger that infuses a man's lust with a powerful surge of energy. Or to put it differently, churches can taboo-charge a man's sexual lust.

Several years ago I spoke on the phone with a national authority in the field of sexually addictive behavior. This psychologist wasn't a Christian, and he didn't know I was. I called him as part of the research for this book. During our conversation he told me something that may surprise you. It did me.

"I believe Christian men are more prone to addictive sexual behavior than any other segment of society."

"Why?" I asked.

"Because churches tend to make sex taboo — especially what it considers deviant sexual behavior. The more forbidden a behavior is, the more excitement it delivers when the taboo is violated. Since most churches don't provide a place for people to talk about their sexual behavior, they can easily become addicted."

Could he be right? Nobody knows for sure. But I'm convinced more Christians are hooked on sexual sins than most of us would imagine. In part, because getting caught doing something sexually off-limits carries greater consequences for a guy who goes to church than for one who doesn't.

Over a period of several years I administered surveys in churches where I conducted seminars. I did this to try and objectify the sexual behavior of Christian men. My aim wasn't to get an absolutely scientific read. I just wanted to get a feel for where the men were coming from. To my surprise, 55 percent of the men surveyed said they struggle, or had struggled in the past, with sexually compulsive behavior.

While many of these men were probably dealing with an occasional battle with pornography and masturbation, others were struggling with more serious compulsions. Make no mistake about it, there are countless men attending church every week who live with the fear they'll be discovered. When the evening news shows pictures of men being arrested for picking up streetwalkers, they cringe in fear. Why? Because just the week before they had cruised the same neighborhood. Like my friend whose story I told at the beginning of this chapter, they know the news story could have been about them.

Risking It All

Sex is a favorite topic of afternoon talk shows. Even the big-name stars of cable news will eagerly host a story about a man who sacrificed everything for a sexual fling. The question they always ask is, "Why did you do it?"

After the Bill Clinton/Monica Lewinsky fiasco, I emailed Bill O'Reilly's producer and said, "I can tell you why President Clinton had sex with Monica Lewinsky in the White House." Two days later I appeared on *The O'Reilly Factor*. The essence of my explanation was that a man must increase the risk to get the rush. What would be riskier for a sitting president than to have sex with a female intern in the White House?

One reason men take such risks is because they're hooked on adrenaline. To get an adrenaline rush, they have to increase the risk. When they were kids, just reading a *Playboy* magazine or surfing the Internet provided enough risk. After all, what would happen if their parents caught them? Now that they're adults, magazines or the digital images on the Internet don't provide enough danger. They need to put all the chips on the table. They need to do something that will cost them dearly if they get caught.

A He-Man with a She-Weakness

God gives us an example in his Word of what can happen when sexual lust runs away with a man's life. If you know anything about Samson (and who doesn't), you know he was strong — freakishly strong. He was faster than Forrest Gump and tougher than Rocky. One day he chased down three hundred foxes, tied their tails together, and lit them on fire. On another occasion he ripped a lion apart with his bare hands. And he struck terror in the hearts of his enemies when he single-handedly killed a thousand Philistines using only a donkey's jawbone.

Samson possessed the kind of physical strength that only comes from God. He was "set apart to God from birth" (Judges 13:5 NIV). The Lord had a purpose for Samson's life, and he wanted people to know about it. That's why Samson never cut his long, flowing locks. His hair wasn't a fashion statement, but a reminder to people of his uncut commitment to God.

Samson had it made. He possessed size, strength, fame, and a tight friendship with God. And he could have had any unmarried woman in Israel (Judges 14:3). Yet Samson craved taboo sex. And that single flaw in his character proved to be his downfall. Listen to his first recorded words: "I have seen a Philistine woman in Timnah; now get her for me as my wife" (Judges 14:2 NIV).

How did his parents respond to that request? They pleaded with him to reconsider. They found it incredible that he couldn't find a godly woman among his relatives ... a woman God would endorse. But Samson craved forbidden fruit, and so he found a nasty girl among his enemies. His logic was simple: "She looks good to me" (Judges 14:3 NASB).

Of course, marrying the Philistine woman would mean turning his back on God and his family. If that was the price, he would willingly pay it. As strong as he was, Samson couldn't break the grip of his sexual desires.

Tragically, Samson's marriage to the Philistine was cut short by her death.

Afterward he seemed to have bridled his sexual appetite for twenty years. But as he approached his fortieth birthday, his appetite broke free. Like a pig pulled into muck, so Samson's sexual compulsions pulled him into the arms of another Philistine woman, Delilah.

Once his appetite for taboo sex took over, he refused to stop until he got what he wanted. And the price proved high. He lost his hair, a symbol of his friendship with God. He lost his strength. He lost his reputation as a powerful and godly warrior. And when the Philistines realized his weakness, they gouged out his eyes — never would he look at one of their women again. Finally, he died among the Philistines.

From the story of Samson
we find out what happens
when good men are tempted
without a plan for victory.

The Temptation Cycle

The silver lining in Samson's story is that we can discover how he fell and avoid a similar flameout. I've broken down his fall into the four stages of the temptation cycle — or what psychologists call the "addictive" cycle.

STAGE ONE: **Preoccupation**

Just as an out-of-shape and overweight middle-aged man is a prime candidate for a heart attack, so Samson was primed to commit a serious sexual sin. He had just turned forty and stood on top of the food chain. He had crushed the Philistines and ruled Israel for twenty years. As often happens to men who achieve such success, he lacked a vision for the rest of his life, something to stoke his fires. And so he got bored. Before long the boredom degraded into a mild state of depression.

Without an enemy to conquer, the world's strongest man grew vulnerable to something that would create a mood swing — make him feel better. And nothing could change his mood like a beautiful woman — especially a sexy Philistine woman. Like the one he enjoyed two decades before. I suspect just the thought released enough adrenaline to lift his mood. Before long he spent hours daydreaming about his previous sexual adventures. He fantasized about an exciting night with one of the prostitutes in Philistia.

Eventually he traveled to Gaza. He may have reasoned that he was "just checking things out." Soon he wandered into the red-light district. When he returned home he had new fuel for his sexual fantasies. Now he had the faces and figures of the women he had seen. Now he could imagine the details of seducing them.

Preoccupation is easy to minimize. After all, it seems harmless enough. After all, what damage can be done by just thinking about having sex with an attractive and available woman? You know, someone like the girl at the gym or at work or at church? While that reasoning may seem valid, we don't want to forget that our thoughts are seeds that germinate and grow into actions that are hard to kill. And we don't want to forget that Jesus condemned adultery of the heart (Matthew 5:28).

STAGE TWO: **Ritualization**

Rituals are activities that put feet on our fantasies. They're a process we repeatedly perform before we act on our compulsions. When something excites us, we do it over and over again. We ritualize it.

For Samson, the rituals may have involved making return trips to Gaza or flirting with the prostitutes — something to get him close to the action to help him feel the rush of sexual excitement. I would imagine Samson struggled with his conscience. No wonder! He was Israel's spiritual leader. How did he justify his actions? He probably told himself Jewish women weren't exciting enough for a man like him. And besides, with his God-given sex drive, how could one woman be expected to satisfy him?

He may have convinced himself he wasn't doing anything wrong — after all, he wasn't having sex with these women. Technically speaking, he hadn't committed adultery. But man, was he ever inching closer to the line. Just like guys today who move from preoccupation to the ritualization of their sexual compulsions.

Does this discussion make you wonder if you have rituals? Maybe it's channel surfing late at night or browsing through a magazine rack in a book store or entering certain words into the search engine of your computer or flirting with an attractive woman at work.

It's crucial for you to know that once you start a ritual you will act on your sexual compulsion. It's certain.

STAGE THREE: **Acting Out**

Finally, during one of his trips, Samson stepped over the line. He slept with a Philistine prostitute (Judges 16:1). After resisting the urge for so long — after playing around with the idea for months or years — he gave in. Resting in the woman's arms, Samson felt alive, more alive than he had felt in years. He had regained the exhilaration of young love. And all he had to do to get such a powerful mood swing was unbridle his lust and let it run wild.

STAGE FOUR: **Shame**

No matter how great the pleasure, his conscience began to accuse him. How could a man of God sleep with a prostitute? How could he risk his reputation? How could he have ignored his friendship with God?

Judges 16:3 gives us a clue regarding his feelings after he slept with the hooker. Samson had entered her home boldly in the light of day. He didn't care who saw him. But after the deed had been done, he slithered out under cover of darkness, hoping nobody would see him. And while Samson might have escaped the woman's presence, he couldn't run away from his shame.

Repeat Performance

After that single night with the prostitute, Samson probably vowed to stay away from Gaza. Maybe you've made a similar vow after masturbating while watching a porn flick in a hotel room or spending time visiting porn sites on the Internet. If so then you understand the shame Samson felt. And you may also know that when the pain of boredom or depression or stress returns, so does your preoccupation with sex, your tendency to perform rituals and your certain repeated fall into sexual sins followed by a new wave of shame.

That's what happened to Samson. After crossing the line his sexual cravings intensified and crossing it again proved easier. That's why he returned to Gaza and slept with Delilah.

The story of Samson's sexual exploits illustrates the danger of repeating the four-stage temptation cycle. When the cycle is repeated —

- The craving for sex intensifies
- The craving for risk intensifies
- The desire to resist weakens

> *Like a deadly whirlpool that pulls*
> *under even the strongest man,*
> *the temptation cycle will drag you down.*

Later I'll share with you a strategy for breaking the temptation cycle. This plan is so important I'm convinced it will give victory to the new man — the good man — within you the next time you're tempted.

Before we get to that plan we need to not only understand the temptation cycle, which explains *what* we do, but we need to understand *why* we get hooked on sexual sins. If you're ready to make that discovery, turn the page.

FOR DISCUSSION

1. In what ways do Christian churches and groups sometimes create an atmosphere that intensifies the problem of sexual lust?

2. In what way does the other woman give the illusion of intimacy? How does that illusion differ from real intimacy?

3. How can connecting with his wife and other men help a man deal with that illusion?

4. What are the four stages of the temptation cycle? How is the cycle dangerous once a man steps into it?

5. What are rituals? What are some of yours?

6. Just as Satan glamorizes the beauty of a woman who is off-limits, so God can enable a man to see his wife's beauty. Ask God to help you do that.

The Thrill
of Young Love

Phoenix is as beautiful in the winter as it is ugly in the summer.

In the winter the weather is dry and moderate and sunny and much better than the rain in Portland, Oregon, where I live. A kaleidoscope of desert flowers laugh at the ever-shining but never-burning winter sun. The cheerful flowers wave at the wind that dances playfully through their pedicels. People wearing bright-colored shirts and jeans eat at outside tables that are round and rest on flat, tan patio stones that come from Mexico. Patio umbrellas aren't needed because everyone loves the sun and welcomes its gentle touch on their face and arms. Everyone is happy. And they laugh because they are superior to those miserable people living in the awful frozen parts of the world ... especially northern Michigan, and upstate New York.

That's Phoenix in the winter. The day I'm here it's summer. The sun laughs maliciously at the arrogant, and now dead, flowers. Its scorching noontime heat melts away the smiling face from anybody unable or unwilling to travel to happy places up north where it's cool, flowers, grow, and people sit outside and eat on tiled patios. The blistering hot wind shoots superheated particles of red-glowing dust against cars and signs and walls, and forces people to wear robes made of Kevlar — the material used in body armor.

I'm in Phoenix in the summer, and it's not like Phoenix in the winter. Every creature is either inside, trying to get inside, dying, or dead.

The good news is I got a great "summer rate" on my motel room. The bad news is I'm depressed. But then I see that my television has something like four thousand channels. Maybe it's four hundred. Whatever ... it's plenty to keep me busy. And so I'm sitting in a crummy air-conditioned, white-walled, shag-carpeted, nicotine-scented room, with the shades drawn, channel surfing.

And now I see an image that increases my heart rate ... a very pretty, perfectly shaped, and partially dressed female dancer. Like the night I gazed at my neighbor through her window, I'm captivated. I do not turn off the television. I do not unplug the set. Instead, I sit and channel surf.

While the temptation cycle, which we saw in the last chapter, explains what men do, it doesn't explain *why* they get hooked on compulsive masturbation or other sexual activities. Uncovering the "why?" isn't easy, because different things cause men to become sexually compulsive. Yet there are at least four common threads of distorted thinking in each story of sexual compulsion.

"I Can Recreate the Thrill of Young Love"

Looking back on that experience I realize why it affected me so strongly. Before that moment in Arizona I could only remember seeing a single pornographic image in the previous twenty years. I had guarded my eyes so diligently that I refused to allow any erotic images past the gate. Like a double shot of whisky to a teetotaler, what I saw carried a powerful punch.

When I returned to my home in Portland, I discussed my experience with my band of brothers. By that time I was hunting for an insight beyond the beauty of a woman's naked body to explain what I feared could become a growing sexual compulsion. I was experiencing some powerful emotions and wanted to root out their source. As my buddies talked about similar experiences they'd had, I realized that the feelings we all described were like those of an infatuated teenager. It seemed like viewing porn recreated the thrill of young love.

We laughed as we talked about our first love. There's something about a man's first love that sets it apart. You know what I mean? The first passionate kiss. The first caress of … well, you get the idea. Young love awakened feelings and unleashed emotions that were new and raw and powerful. It opened a new and unexplored world.

Of course, first loves seldom last. My first girlfriend and I broke up, and a couple of years later I met Cindy. We fell in love, and once more I experienced the exhilaration of infatuation or love or whatever you want to call it. During our courtship I was drunk on love.

And I'm blessed because after decades of marriage, we still love each other. Mature love is deeper and truer than young love. But it seldom provides the "thrill of young love." In fact, while I hate to admit it, there are times when I feel as much romantic love for Cindy as I would for one of my sisters.

A lot of guys think that feelings of romantic love are the true measure of love. Consequently, because they seldom have such feelings for their wife they conclude they must not be in love at all. Over time, they feel as dead emotionally as a cadaver. And then suddenly, and maybe even unexpectedly, they see a pornographic image on their computer monitor. Or a pretty and flirtatious coworker places a hand on their shoulder and asks them out for lunch. Instantly, they experience an emotional resurrection. The long-lost and almost-forgotten thrill of young love is theirs again. Like a teenager about to cross the line and kiss his girl for the first time, they feel excited, nervous, and alive.

So why do you find yourself repeatedly pulled back to porn sites or illicit affairs? Because you've discovered how you can once again, regardless of your age or marital status, experience the thrill of young love. But there's a problem.

The Law of Diminishing Returns

Men who get turned on by porn will find that what once aroused them quickly becomes routine. Looking at a girl in a bikini soon leads to more images, which leads to video clips. This happens because sexual sins involve the law of diminishing returns. Which means it takes more and more stimulation to get the same degree of pleasure. Remember that first kiss and how quickly you wanted to move from the lips to the breasts. Sexual sins are progressive because each experience seems less exciting than what comes next — or what a man hopes will come next.

Once a man has seduced a woman, he has planted the flag. She is his — at least for the moment. The hunt, or pursuit, is over. If you're a single guy, I've got some disappointing news for you. Many married men consider their sex life boring. Why? Because they've progressed as far with their wife as they can. There's no challenge. There's no new terrain to explore. Even in the best of marriages, with the best possible sex, men still periodically struggle with such feelings.

My experience in Phoenix excited me like my first-grade crush on Cynthia Russell, the affection I felt for my high school sweetheart, and the crazy love I had for Cindy. And like a kid in love, I wanted more. Of course, I faced a grave danger. To get the same rush, I would have to progress. The thrill of young love could be mine, but I'd have to view more explicit images. Eventually they too would become boring and to recreate the thrill I'd have to move on to something more illicit and dangerous.

Fortunately, I cut the process off before it went any further. But not everyone makes that choice. The hunt for young love involves the law of diminishing returns that drives men to progressively increase the risk.

When women ask me, "Why is my husband so attracted to pornography?" I ask them, "Do you remember as a teenager when you first fell in love? Do you remember how good it felt to be with your boyfriend? Do you remember how you wanted to be with him all the time?"

Most women smile and say they remember. "That's how your husband feels about pornography," I tell them. "It gives him the thrill of young love."

"Identity Theft"

In the pursuit of illicit pleasure something bad happens to a man. His self-image changes — or reverts back to how he saw himself before he became a Christian. If he's growing spiritually then he's beginning to see himself as a new man in Christ. He — that is the new and good man God has changed him into — has tapped into the power of God through the Holy Spirit. But once he begins to masturbate in front of his computer monitor, visit strip clubs, or cheat on his wife with other women, he unleashes his sin with its lustful appetites and before long the lust-driven thoughts and actions define his person. In a sense, his sin has stolen his identity away from the new and good man God made him when he trusted in Christ.

This sense of self-hatred and shame produces an increased level of emotional pain which the man then has to work harder to deaden. One thing is certain: after a man gives in to his sexual compulsions long enough, he loses sight of the new man he's become in Christ and sees himself, not as a son of God, but as an immoral man.

Sadly, once he sees himself this way, acting out is easier. After all, he may say, "It's just the way I am." His sexual behavior is consistent with his current low self-worth, which is based on the cravings of his lower sinful thoughts and behaviors.

These feelings of unworthiness may be fed by childhood experiences and memories. In the Old Testament, God repeatedly warned the Israelites that he would visit the sins of the fathers upon their children (Exodus 20:5; Numbers 14:18). Nowhere is this more apparent than in the area of sexual compulsions.

I don't take the Old Testament warning to mean that there is an inherited generational tendency that, like an unbroken chain, must link a man's behavior to his father. Rather, I think the dad models sexual behavior that a son will tend to follow. I've had numerous men who struggle with porn tell me they first saw it while reading a magazine belonging to their father, grandfather, uncle, or other family member. Often they would masturbate while looking at the erotic images. Later, they would feel guilty and ashamed and tell themselves they are bad. Not only does the attraction to pornography carry over into adult life, so does the shame.

Some men suffered sexual abuse as children. Even though they did nothing wrong, they may have a deep sense of emotional dirtiness and shame that triggers a fear that those they love will abandon them. One reason they fear abandonment is because parents who abused them may have threatened to leave if they told their secret. Researchers Eist and Mandel note that within families in which incest has occurred, "Tremendous parental threats of abandonment were a most frequent technique employed by the parent to control or immobilize their children."[1]

Boys who fear desertion feel unwanted. It's easy for them to think if they're unwanted they must be bad. And bad men do bad things … bad sexual things.

"No One Would Love Me If They Really Knew Me"

Because men feel safe with me, they frequently tell me things they're ashamed of. After listening to a painful confession, I'll frequently ask, "Have you told anyone else?" Usually they'll answer with a simple "No."

When I ask why, I'm told they don't have a friend, including their wife, who could handle it. They keep it to themselves to avoid rejection. They can't imagine someone loving a person so impure, defiled, and perverted. Such feelings may cause a man to conclude:

- Real people can't be trusted
- Real people won't meet their needs
- Real people bring rejection and pain

Since such men feel unworthy of love by real people, it makes sense they would settle for an illusion of love. In contrast to the suffering caused by real people, pornography and masturbation provide pleasure without the risk of rejection. The image on the Internet never lets them down. It always gives a mood swing. It always brings pleasure. It always gives the illusion of intimacy.

"Sex Is My Most Important Need"

Men who grew up in abusive families sometimes turned to masturbation as a means of nurturing themselves. In a world of pain, they found something that made them feel better. Often the compulsive or habitual nature of their masturbation would reflect the emotional pain they were suffering. The greater the emotional pain, the stronger the drive to masturbate.

As boys, they equated sexual pleasure with love, care, and safety. As adults, whenever they experience pain they immediately turn to sexual pleasure as a means of coping and proving to themselves that they're okay.

For such men, nothing in life is more important than sex. They didn't bond with their parents when growing up, they bonded with sexual pleasure. Such guys put their need for sex above the needs, wishes, or desires of their wife. Sex comes before God and work. Nothing is more important than sex because sex drives away pain and replaces it with pleasure.

Getting Out of the Trap

I've never found it helpful to be given a formula for sexual purity and told to, "Just follow the directions." When I first learned that I gravitated toward sexual sins I wanted to understand why. I wanted to discover how my thinking got distorted so I could correct it. I hope as you've read this chapter, and the previous one, you've gained a better understanding of compulsive sexual behavior and the distorted thinking behind it. But you may wonder exactly how serious a problem you have. And you may want to know how you can find freedom.

In the next chapter you'll discover the scope of your problem, and you'll learn how you can pry open the teeth of the trap, pull out your soul, and take the first step toward allowing the good man in you to live a life of freedom.

FOR DISCUSSION

1. How does sexual impurity involve the law of diminishing returns? Can you think of a time when you experienced this?

2. In what way does an off-limits sexual experience create the illusion of young love? What must a man do to keep that illusion alive?

3. Why would a man hooked on impure sex feel that others wouldn't love him if they really knew him?

4. When a man feels he's unlovable how does that drive him to act out sexually?

5. Read Psalm 32 (the NIV version is reprinted below) and reflect on how God deals with a man who confesses his sins (David had committed adultery and murder). Write out some of your observations. What does God's treatment of David tell you about how he will respond when you confess your sins to him?

   > *Blessed is he*
   >   *whose transgressions are forgiven,*
   >   *whose sins are covered.*
   > *Blessed is the man*
   >   *whose sin the LORD does not count against him*
   >   *and in whose spirit is no deceit.*
   > *When I kept silent,*
   >   *my bones wasted away*
   >   *through my groaning all day long.*

For day and night
   your hand was heavy upon me;
   my strength was sapped
   as in the heat of summer.
Then I acknowledged my sin to you
   and did not cover up my iniquity.
   I said, "I will confess
   my transgressions to the LORD" —
   and you forgave
   the guilt of my sin.
Therefore let everyone who is godly pray to you
   while you may be found;
   surely when the mighty waters rise,
   they will not reach him.
You are my hiding place;
   you will protect me from trouble
   and surround me with songs of deliverance.
I will instruct you and teach you in the way you should go;
   I will counsel you and watch over you.
Do not be like the horse or the mule,
   which have no understanding
   but must be controlled by bit and bridle
   or they will not come to you.
Many are the woes of the wicked,
   but the LORD's unfailing love
   surrounds the man who trusts in him.
Rejoice in the LORD and be glad, you righteous;
   sing, all you who are upright in heart!

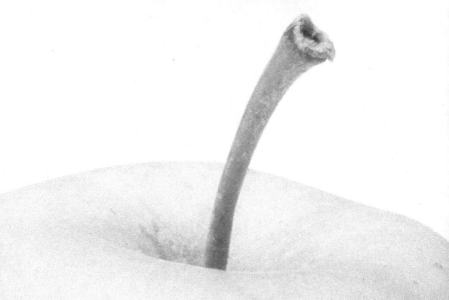

PART TWO

ADMITTING THE STRUGGLE

How Big Is Your Problem?

When I was a kid my dad never bragged about his grades. I guess that's because he never finished high school. He grew up with a family of nine kids on a farm in west Texas. He learned at an early age that he had a talent for inflicting bodily pain on people. His talent probably resulted from his Popeye-sized arms that he developed as a boy while milking cows every morning. While he never played professional football he did play high school ball until he was twenty. He said back then school took longer because you had to skip classes to do farm work.

Even though he never finished high school or played pro football, he was a professional boxer, and he made a lot of money selling life insurance to west Texas oilmen and ranchers. They liked his earthy style.

Anyway, I've told you that so you'll understand why as a boy I never gave any attention to my homework, and why I didn't place much value on behaving in class, and why I liked to get in fights, and why I seemed to get in a fight just about every week.

Dad took pride in my scrappy nature. He seldom asked how I was doing in school, but he always wanted to know if I had gotten into any fights. (In case you haven't guessed, my dad had some strange values.) He loved to brag about what a tough kid I was. I remember hearing him talk to his friends about my street-fighting skill. He boasted about how I could whip a kid I knew would kill me if we ever got in a fight. Of course, I realized I lacked the speed, strength, and mean streak that made my dad such a ferocious fighter. And I knew that I tried to fight only kids I could beat.

At an early age I learned from my dad: "Don't ever give up. Let them knock you out, but don't give up. If they kick you, gouge out your eyes, bite off an ear, chew off your nose, or break your arm — don't give up."

The one fight I lost in grade school I lost long before I had lost my eyes or nose or an ear or suffered a broken bone. But I didn't give up until I knew without a doubt there was no way I would win. Then and only then did I surrender to a superior force.

Of course, most of us won't capitulate until we know we're defeated or we see defeat coming as fast and certain as a freight train. That's one reason a lot of guys wait until their sexual behavior causes their world to crash in around them before they admit they're fighting an enemy they can't overpower.

Scouting Report

With that reality in mind, you can see why it's crucial for you to size up your enemy before you step back into the ring. You need to know how much domination your sexual compulsions are exerting over your life.

To help you do that I've prepared a scouting report that consists of four questions. They're designed to help you determine the seriousness of your problem. If you're not going to be brutally honest, don't bother answering the questions —

because it won't do you any good. You can just skip to the next chapter. On the other hand, if you've got a problem, you need to know it and admit it. Why wait until you've lost an eye or ear or suffered a broken bone to admit you're fighting an opponent you can't beat alone?

1. Is Your Behavior a Secret?

Are you doing things you refuse to tell others about? Do you fear if those closest to you knew what you were up to, they'd reject you or disapprove (that is, *adamantly* and with *strong emotion*) of your actions? Are you telling lies to cover your behavior? If so, you're isolating yourself from those you love and entering into a potentially addictive relationship with an object or experience. And you're doing it without seriously considering the long-term consequences of your actions.

2. Is Your Behavior Abusive?

Does your sexual behavior create pain (emotional or physical) for you or others? Is it degrading or exploitative of others? Do you get off on porn that exploits young women?

Do you find yourself performing increasingly abusive acts? Do you derive pleasure from watching others being abused in some way? I'm not just talking about watching an S&M show. Abuse can occur when a young woman's financial needs or ignorance makes her a prime candidate for those in the porn industry to use her for profit. Such a woman is being abused.

3. Is Your Behavior Used to Deaden Painful Feelings?

Are your sexual actions an effort to change your mood rather than express affection? Do you masturbate or search for some other sexual outlet when you're depressed, bored, or angry?

Using masturbation to erase pain or create a mood swing can fuel a sexual addiction.

4. Is Your Behavior Empty of Genuine Commitment and Caring?

Are you substituting the illusion of intimacy provided by pornography and masturbation — or some other form of sinful sexual behavior — for the genuine intimacy found in a healthy relationship?[1]

If you answered yes to even one of the four questions you've got a big-time fight going on in your life. Of course, you probably already knew that. Maybe what you'd like to know is what round you're in ... how much of a beating you've taken.[2]

What Round Are You In?

Because the purpose of this chapter is to help you assess your current situation, you not only need to know if you've got a problem, but you also need to know how far it's progressed. Through research I've discovered that the fight with sexual immorality can last up to five rounds. It's a fight that never ends in a decision if it makes it to the final round.

ROUND ONE: **The Warm-up**

The first round describes men who have recently discovered they get turned on big time by things like viewing porn or visiting strip clubs. If you're in this round then your life's pretty much under control. You're having fun with your new sexual experiences, and you're holding down your job and everything appears cool with your wife or girlfriend.

You know you've endured some pretty powerful punches, however, and your fascination with porn, strip clubs, or dirty talk lines, while not compulsive, is dangerous. You're likely troubled by the fear that your awakened sexual lust is about to take over your life.

In round one a man usually won't tell anyone because he thinks he's got the fight under control. He figures there's no need to risk upsetting his wife or hurting his reputation when he's not in trouble. If you're in the ministry, the drive to cover your tracks may seem especially compelling because your job may be at risk.

ROUND TWO: **The Dragon Emerges**

During round two a man's lust has begun to exert its control and he can't resist his sexual urges. He's *compulsively* involved in such things as masturbation, pornography, homosexuality, or demeaning heterosexual relationships.

When a man reaches round two the most significant thing that happens is the emergence of what some psychologists call the addictive personality.[3] Biblically speaking, he's become a slave of sin (Romans 6:16). Before he struggled to keep his lust under control, now it's running wild. A man's lust, like a rapacious dragon, has awakened from its slumber and threatens to swallow his life. I experienced this the night I looked through my neighbor's window. It reminded me of the first time I got high on marijuana. After a few hits from a joint, I entered a wanton world that I later craved to revisit.

There's something about that first high that people want to re-create. Similarly, a man who enters round two awakens powerful desires, and his lustful cravings ache to re-create that initial experience. When we enter round two the addictive part of our personality has stormed out of its corner — and make no mistake about it, the beast seeks total domination of your life.

ROUND THREE: **The Lawbreaker Emerges**

If a man makes it to round three he's taken a bigger and more dangerous step. Now his behavior involves victims and violations of the law. His activities include prostitution, exhibitionism, voyeurism, obscene phone calls, and touching a person intimately without consent. Most of the time he's considered more of a nuisance than a criminal, but his annoying behavior can inflict deep emotional pain on his victims.

All kinds of good men reach round three. Hardly a week passes without a news story about a politician, teacher, professional athlete, or Hollywood star picking up a prostitute or making an unwanted sexual advance. If you take a moment to recall the past year, I suspect you can remember the name of a high-profile Christian leader whose illegal sexual behavior brought down his ministry and deeply wounded his family.

ROUND FOUR: **The Criminal Emerges**

By the time a man reaches round four he's no longer just a lawbreaker, he's a serious criminal committing severe crimes against his victims. Rape, incest, and child molestation occur at this level.

ROUND FIVE: **The Knockout Punch**

By now you know which round you're in. While most men would prefer avoiding reality for as long as possible, eventually the moment of truth will arrive. Something will happen to force you to admit that your life is out of control. An event will knock you to the canvas with such force you'll wonder if you'll ever get up again.

- You'll accidentally leave a pornographic image on your computer monitor, and someone at work will report it to your boss.

- One of your kids will find your stash of X-rated videos.

- A policeman will arrive at your place of work because a neighbor has identified you as a Peeping Tom.

- Your wife will leave because you've had another affair.

- The school counselor will call because you've been reported to the childcare agency for improperly touching a neighbor child.

- Chris Hansen will step into the room and announce that you're on *Dateline: To Catch a Predator*.

For Samson, the moment of truth arrived near the end of his life. Blinded by lust, he slept in Delilah's lap while a Philistine barber cut his hair. A moment after the last strand fell — and with it, God's power in his life — Samson's enemies stepped into the ring. Isolated from God, he couldn't fight off their attack. Israel's champion became a blind and bald-headed clown who entertained his enemies, the Philistines (Judges 16:20 – 21).

Many people believe Samson's story ends on a tragic note. It doesn't. Although gaping eye sockets boasted ugly scars and strong chains secured his wrists and ankles, Samson's hair began to grow. That single phrase speaks volumes about the spiritual condition of the former champion. The author of Judges didn't care about Samson's appearance. He cared about his friendship with God. The fact that his hair was growing indicated Samson's friendship with God was reviving — growing — getting strong again. The Lord forgave Samson and used him one last time. Empowered once more by God, the hero of Judah pulled down a heavily populated Philistine temple, destroying more enemies in his death than he had over the course of his life.

Samson learned firsthand what every man must know: God is the God of a second and third and fourth chance. He never gives up on us. No matter which round you're in, or how many punches you've taken, or how many times you've been knocked down — God will never give up on you. He's in your corner. But to experience his grace, you must first recognize your need. You must turn to him and others for help. That's not easy. Perhaps you realize you have a problem but still believe you can handle it alone. As I mentioned at the beginning of this chapter, guys hate to admit defeat.

If what you've read so far in this chapter hasn't convinced you that you're fighting a losing battle against a ruthless and oppressive opponent, maybe a few words from the Bible will help. In the next chapter, you'll discover how a great man of God did in his battle against sin. Hint: he didn't win until he realized he couldn't win alone.

FOR DISCUSSION

1. Why is it a good idea to know how serious your problem is and how far it's progressed?

2. What four things indicate a man has a serious problem? As you review these indicators, what do you learn about yourself?

3. What characterizes each round of a sexual sin? What round are you in? Why?

4. What makes round two so dangerous?

5. Why do you want to avoid round five?

6. What does Samson's final act tell you about God? How does that affect you?

Three Ways
to Lose the Battle

I found it hard to believe that my friend, an intelligent, well-educated, professional man, would make such a hare-brained statement. As a petroleum engineer he made big bucks anticipating problems before they occurred at oil-drilling sites in places like Texas, Louisiana, Alaska, and South America. He's the kind of man I expected to have a knack for knowing what could go wrong, and yet, he had just said, "Bill, I don't think I could ever commit a serious sexual sin. You know, like adultery."

I had no idea what prompted him to suddenly make such a ludicrous declaration — we weren't even talking about sex. So I gazed at him for a moment to see if he was kidding. When he maintained the stoic style of a mortician managing a funeral, I knew he meant business.

"If what you're saying is true," I said, "then you're godlier than David — the godliest man in the Old Testament; stronger than Samson — the strongest man in the Old Testament; and wiser than Solomon — the wisest man in the Old Testament."

My friend stared at me for a long time, unsure what to say. Finally, he pushed his horn-rimmed glasses up on his bulbous nose, tilted his stout head to the right, and said, "I never thought about it like that."

Actually, until that moment neither had I. Yet the more I think about it the more I suspect if David, Samson, or Solomon could talk to us today, they would insist we should never underestimate the power of sexual lust, and they would probably urge us never to believe for a moment that we could outrun, outsmart, or overwhelm our sexual lust once it's taken hold of our lives.

The purpose of the previous chapter was to help you assess the seriousness of your problem and determine how far it's progressed. In this chapter I'd like you to consider three biblical insights from the apostle Paul, insights that explain why the methods you may be using to control your lust aren't working well. Or, to look at it from a different angle, these are insights that will tell you three ways to lose the battle against sexual lust every time.

FAILED BATTLE PLAN ONE: **Overpower Your Lust**

If you're discouraged because you've repeatedly broken your promise to stop your compulsive and sinful sexual behavior, then take heart. The apostle Paul understood your predicament. He told the Romans, "I have the desire to do what is good, but I cannot carry it out. For what I do is not the good I want to do; no, the evil I do not want to do — this I keep on doing" (Romans 7:18–19 NIV).

Like the rest of us, Paul struggled with sin. And like the rest of us, he would make up his mind not to commit a certain sin ever again. Did he succeed? No way! Now, if the apostle Paul couldn't overpower his sinful appetites, what chance do we have?

Suppose you made up your mind you were going to make it through one day without lusting after a woman. On your way to work your eyes are drawn to the bikini-clad model greeting you from a billboard. You tell yourself you won't look, but your lust takes over and you feel a mild and pleasurable rush of adrenaline and endorphins.

A few moments later as you stop at an intersection a luscious young woman wearing skin-tight shorts, very short shorts, walks directly into your line of sight. You again tell yourself, "I shouldn't stare at her," but staring feels good. So you don't look away until the light turns green and the driver behind you honks his horn breaking your trance.

At work a friend brags about the gorgeous babe he bedded the night before. You know you shouldn't listen to the details, but you do.

As you order lunch, the waitress with the short skirt and plunging neckline that reveals her — okay, you get the idea. Anyway, she winks at you and you don't want to flirt, but flirting feels good and besides, your wife's not with you. Each time the waitress walks by you peek at her best features, and she looks at you with a playful smile.

When you get back to the office, you discover that a friend has emailed you a picture of his favorite erotic image. You know you shouldn't open it. You tell yourself not to. But the power of your lust is too strong, and so you open the picture and let your lust wallow in the warmth of her beauty.

On your way home you stop at the grocery store and don't even try to look away from the images of the seminude models that adorn the magazines by the checkout counter.

When you finally arrive home, you plop down into an easy chair and flip on the TV. As you channel surf, you know which channels to avoid. But nobody's home and you can't resist the urge to search for a flick with some exposed female flesh.

Okay, you could play make-believe and pretend you're so spiritual you never ever even notice a beautiful woman. But in the real world, answer these questions: With the high level of erotic stimulation you face on a daily basis, do you believe you can bridle your lust alone? How successful have you been in the past? And if the past is an indicator of the future, how well do you think you'll do tomorrow and the day after that?

FAILED BATTLE PLAN TWO: Reform Your Lust

About now you may be thinking, "Maybe I can't overpower my lust, but I can sure reform it. I can make myself better."

As I mentioned before, I sometimes talk with new Christians who think that becoming a follower of Christ means their lust problem is solved. It's as though they think Jesus waved a magic wand over them and — presto! — he eradicated their sinful appetites.

When they discover their problem with lust seems worse than before, they decide they'll study the Bible and pray more. Much to their surprise, that doesn't solve the problem either.

Undaunted, they decide to memorize a verse like Job 31:1 (NIV), "I made a covenant with my eyes not to look lustfully at a girl." And they promise God, and themselves, that they will never gaze lustfully at any woman or erotic image of a woman. And guess what? That doesn't work either. In fact, none of their spiritual exercises provide them with long-term victory. So, like a lot of Christian guys, they just give up. Or they keep trying and failing, all the while pretending they've got their sexual lust under control — just like other Christian guys.

Listen to Paul's words. In Romans 7:10 – 11 he said, "The very command that was supposed to guide me into life was cleverly used to trip me up, throwing me headlong."[1]

Our lustful appetites are so evil they'll use God's commands to tempt us. Like a rod stirring up dirt that has settled to the bottom of a jar of water, God's law stirs up our lust. As we've seen, women who are off-limits look better. God says "don't" and our lust says "do." God says "do" and our lust says "don't."

Trying to reform our lust
is like trying to make a dog into a person.

For thirteen years a buff-colored cocker spaniel named Pumpkin graced our family. Over those years I taught Pumpkin all kinds of tricks. She obeyed the common commands like sit, lie down, and roll over. I also trained her to jump through a hoop, close a door, sit on her hind legs, and fall over as though dead when I shot her with an imaginary gun.

Yet in spite of all my training, I couldn't keep Pumpkin from acting like a dog. She always did doggy things. She ate poop as though it was steak. She sniffed other dog's butts as though they were roses. She went to the bathroom on public sidewalks. No matter how well I trained Pumpkin, she was still a dog. The bottom line is — you never take the dog out of a dog.

Similarly, you never take the sin out of a sinner. Your sinful appetites don't go away or get better when you enter a church. They don't change when you come to faith in Christ. You can go to church, read your Bible, pray daily, and even lead a ministry without, in the least bit, reforming your sinful appetites.

Paul put it this way, "For I know that nothing good dwells in me, that is, in my flesh; for the willing is present in me, but the doing of the good is not" (Romans 7:18 NASB).

When we fall under the domination of our flesh, that part of our personality that craves gratification apart from God, we're capable of doing anything evil, whether we're believers or not. When controlled by our lust and not God's Spirit working through our new man, we can no more do good deeds than a Poodle can speak French or a Chihuahua speak Spanish.

So a guy who thinks he can reform his lust is denying the essence of his flesh. He's denying the sin that still resides in him.

That doesn't mean you can't grow as a believer. Certainly your spiritual nature, the new you, the good man in you, can grow in Christ. But in the flesh, in your sinful propensity, you'll never get better.

FAILED BATTLE PLAN THREE: Starve Your Lust

One of the problems I have with a lot of recovery programs is that their primary emphasis is on abstinence. They think the key to defeating sexual sins is to stop the behavior. They make their entire plan for sexual purity center around "not looking." Now, don't misunderstand me. We can't control our lust unless we stop gaping at erotic images or sexually attractive women. But if that's all we do, it won't work. We'll either fall back into the behavior we're working so hard to avoid or switch addictions. For example, our lust will transfer from sex to alcohol, and if we stop drinking, it will move on to shopping or work or gambling.

It's impossible to starve our lust to death. Until the day we're with the Lord, and sin resides in us no more, we'll battle with our flesh and the lust it generates. I think I've captured the idea in the following poem.

The Dragon

I found a dragon on my step
Small and agile
Please stay awhile

Every day we'd take a walk
Master and pet
Why the cold sweat?

And then I saw he held the leash
Tall and vile
I've got no file.

I found a dragon on my step
False hearted foe
Who will never let go.

The dragon in your soul, the old and evil man, will resist letting go. For a while you may ignore him. Later you may insist he holds you no longer. But if you hope to break his grip, you must first acknowledge his presence and admit you don't have the power to break free from his leash.

Hopefully, you're tired of fighting a losing battle. Other men, like Paul were. In desperation he cried out, "Oh, what a miserable person I am! Who will free me from this life that is dominated by sin and death?" (Romans 7:24).

If someone as spiritual as Paul realized he was fighting a losing battle against his flesh and its evil desires, isn't it time you reached the same conclusion? I know giving up the fight isn't easy. But giving up the fight in your own strength is the first step to victory.

I hope since you've read this far you understand that the wonderful gift God has given you to appreciate the beauty of a naked woman can easily be distorted by your lust, and I hope you have a clear grasp of the extent of your problem.

I hope you believe you can't win the fight against your lust without a plan that enables you to unleash the new and good man within you to tap into the power of God.

A crucial part of that plan involves dealing with the damage your soul has suffered at the hands of your unbridled lust — damage that your old man, your sinful flesh, will use to create more pain, which could drive you to even more compulsive sexual behavior. In the next chapter we'll look at that pain and how God can heal the wounds that cause it.

FOR DISCUSSION

1. Why can't you overpower or reform your lust?

2. Have you reached the place where you know you can't defeat your lust alone yet? If not, why not? If yes, why?

3. How have you tried to overpower your lustful appetites? How well has it worked out? Why? Why not?

4. How have you tried to reform your lust? Did it work? Why not?

5. Why can't you starve your lustful appetites?

6. What is the advantage of knowing you can't beat your lust through self-effort?

Crawl into the Cave
and Drag Out the Bear

Okay, so I'm standing in front of four hundred high school students in northern California, delivering a message entitled "The Five Misconceptions Regarding Sex." While I don't remember the five misconceptions any more than I remember the names of the last five Super Bowl winners, I remember something that happened during the talk.

The something surprised me because the nature of the topic prompts students to listen with the focused attention they'd normally reserve for their favorite band. Yet as I was speaking some of the kids would laugh at the middle or end of a sentence as though I had just told a joke.

I'd say something like, "The sky is blue," and they'd laugh. Or I'd say something like, "God wants the best for you," and they'd laugh.

Then I realized why they were laughing.

"Oh, no!" I said to myself. "My fly's open."

There I stood with my hands in my pockets, with my barn door open, talking about sex. I knew right away that once the kids saw the humor in the situation they couldn't hold back their laughter. Sensing my confusion and embarrassment more kids joined in the fun.

I suspect you realize people fear public speaking more than heights, bugs, financial loss, sickness, torture, and even death. So how do you think most men would respond if after overcoming their fear of speaking and actually addressing an audience of four hundred people — no, not people, high school students — they realized every kid in the house was staring at their open fly and either laughing or holding back a laugh?

Seeking to subdue my embarrassment and rectify the situation I nonchalantly tried to check my zipper. But how do you do that with four hundred kids watching? I certainly didn't want to grab the zipper for fear I'd look like I was trying to pull off a Michael Jackson, pretrial impersonation. And then I got a brilliant idea: "I'll hold my Bible in front of the barn door so they can't look inside."

I took that defensive stance, but something was wrong — terribly wrong. The kids kept laughing at inappropriate times.

When I finished speaking, while everyone else bowed their heads and closed their eyes and I prayed, I turned away from the crowd and checked my zipper. Hmmm ... it was up. I had clearly endured the mortification of embarrassment for nothing. Then a horrible thought occurred to me: What if they were laughing about something that would cause even more embarrassment? Now, I'm not paranoid, but in that moment I sensed I would soon discover a truth that would cause lifelong humiliation.

After the meeting a handful of students gathered around me and asked questions like, "Can you prove the existence of God? Do aliens exist? How do you resolve the conflict between the goodness of God and the origin of evil?"

After taking a few minutes to answer each of those questions in detail, using words they didn't understand and therefore couldn't argue with, I said, "Now, I've got a question for you." That statement couldn't have gotten their attention more if it had come from a talking cat. "Why were ya'll laughing throughout my talk?"

"Oh," a cute sixteen-year-old girl giggle-gushed, "because of your Texas accent."

I breathed a sigh of relief so great I sensed the loss of air might cause my body to collapse like a deflated parade balloon. "You're sure?" I asked.

"Yeah. I'm sure," she said.

"Oh," I said.

Toxic Shame

While embarrassment is uncomfortable, it's no big deal and it's usually triggered by doing something in front of someone you want to impress. You know, like stumbling or spilling food all over yourself or forgetting someone's name or exposing a sock with a hole in it. The shame associated with such embarrassment is healthy. It reminds us we're human and keeps us from taking ourselves too seriously.

But there's another kind of shame that's toxic. It's like the radioactive waste that's stored in 177 steel-gray tanks buried along the Columbia River in the Pacific Northwest. Some of the containers leaked releasing deadly radioactive material into the ground where it seeped into the river. God didn't design the human soul to serve as a shame container. Eventually toxic shame will leak out destroying a man's sense of self-respect and undermining his ability to build strong friendships.

This shame poisons our identity as men because it's based on the belief that we've failed God and ourselves. And it's different from guilt. Guilt addresses behavior ... what we've done. It's a painful feeling about our actions. If I told a lie, my conscience would bother me because of my misdeed. The feeling of a guilty conscience is healthy, just like the pain caused by a bumped head or stubbed toe. It prompts us to take therapeutic action to facilitate healing and preventative action to protect ourselves in the future.

Shame causes a deeper and more harmful pain than guilt because it's triggered by how we see ourselves, rather than a specific act. It deceives us into seeing ourselves as we once were rather than who we now are in Christ. Unlike guilt that prompts positive steps that stimulate growth and prompts a follower of Christ to remember he's a new man, shame acts like an untreated infection that poisons our soul and cripples our behavior. Because he dislikes who he is, a shameful man resists revealing himself to others and to himself. That last phrase seems strange, doesn't it? But the awful truth is he's afraid to look at himself too closely because he won't like what he sees. Indeed, he may hate what he sees.[1] What he may not realize is that he fears looking at his sin and the evil desires and actions that it generates. It's the sinful dragon in his soul that he hates.

Several years ago my oldest son, Ryan, felt a small growth on his left testicle. His wife, a surgeon, did a quick exam and said, "You've got testicular cancer."*

While that's not the news a man wants to hear, at least it contained a nugget of good news — so to speak — namely, testicular cancer is among the most treatable forms of cancer a man can get. In fact, if it's caught early enough the cure rate

---

* Testicular cancer is treatable. Ryan is cancer free and has fathered a child since the surgery. Young men have a higher risk of testicular cancer. In men, testicular cancer is the most common cancer between the ages of twenty and thirty-four, the second most common cancer between the ages of thirty-five and thirty-nine, and the third most common cancer between the ages of fifteen and nineteen. If you feel something unusual, see your doctor.

approaches 100 percent. A few weeks after the initial detection Ryan had the testicle removed and underwent a series of radiation treatments.

His recovery seemed to be going well and then one day he called me and said, "Dad, I've got an unexpected complication from the surgery."

"What's that, son?"

"When I walk I lean to the right."

As a result of his surgery he's heard some unusual cancer stories. One of the most bizarre concerned a young man whose testicle had grown to the size of a softball before, at his mother's insistence — she could see it bulging through his pants — he finally saw a doctor. Unfortunately, he had waited too long and the cancer killed him.

When Ryan told me that story I couldn't help but wonder why that man would ignore such an obvious and unhealthy change in his anatomy, and then it occurred to me: he probably convinced himself the problem either didn't exist or it would resolve itself without medical attention. That kind of delusional thinking allowed him to avoid the pain of facing the truth about himself — he had cancer. But it also killed him.

Men do that with the toxic shame that resides in their soul. They refuse to experience the mental and emotional pain that would be created by a deep and thoughtful examination of their heart. So, like the man hauling around a huge testicle, they haul around their toxic shame hoping it will just get better. But it doesn't. It just keeps growing like a deadly tumor in their soul.

A man who refuses to look at himself alienates himself from God and other people. But he also finds that a sexual object — or image or experience — can quickly replace his pain and loneliness with pleasure and an illusion of intimacy.

(That last sentence is important and you might want to reread it a few times and let its meaning sink in.)

Unfortunately, every peek at an Internet porn site, every visit to an adult video store, every one-night stand, and every affair only serves to create a greater sense of unworthiness, shame, and self-loathing. This increased shame and pain intensifies the need to sinfully feed the sexual appetite to deaden the pain and replace the feelings of aloneness with false intimacy.

Because I didn't grow up in the mystical town of Pleasantville, where everyone and everything is perfect, by the time I was twenty I had done a lot of regrettable things. What bothered me the most was my inability to make consistently good moral decisions. I believed I had a lot going for me, but I saw myself as morally rotten to the core. So how did I cope with my shame? I smoked dope and chased girls to deaden the pain of my loneliness and hurt. The problem is, the more I acted out with drugs and sex, the more shame I felt and the more dope and sex I needed to feel okay.

When I became a devoted follower of Christ, my lifestyle changed. But my feelings of shame didn't go away like a bad dream upon waking. I remember not wanting to have kids for years after I got married because I feared they'd grow up and be like me. I saw myself as deeply flawed, and even though I wasn't getting stoned and chasing girls, I believed my lust would one day wake up and climb out of bed just like Rip Van Winkle.

Go Into the Cave

Dealing with your feelings of shame is like climbing into a cave with a sleeping bear. The best you can hope for is a bad scare. But if you actually grab hold of the bear, things could get bloody. The bear might use his claws to rip you apart and his jaws to crush your skull. Because most men feel ill-equipped to take on such a dangerous beast they avoid the dark cave and the bear it hides.

While fear can protect us from legitimate danger, it also has the power to keep us from facing the truth about our-selves. Isn't that what happened to Adam and Eve? Before the Fall they were "both naked, and they felt no shame" (Genesis 2:25 NIV). What a statement! They had nothing to hide from each other. Adam and Eve experienced intimacy with God and each other.

I think their personalities, or souls, had a glasslike quality that enabled them to see into each other, and it never occurred to Adam to close the blinds to prevent Eve from observing his deepest thoughts and feelings. He had nothing to hide.

Then sin entered the picture. Their wrongdoing caused them not only to suffer guilt but to become spiritually scarred. Their formerly perfect souls now carried a vile flaw, like a baby's unblemished skin that is touched with a white-hot branding iron, leaving it with an ugly and painful wound that would turn into an unsightly and unfeeling scar. But their misdeed had gone deeper than the skin. It had left its hideous mark on their soul.

Or to put it differently, it had changed the very root of the tree. No longer was the root good and healthy, it was now evil and sick. The essence of their character had changed. They had become sinners from the heart.

How did they respond to that reality? They feared God. They feared he would see that their misdeed had given birth to sin — it had changed the essence of their being. They feared he would see the ugly dragon in their soul and reject them. So they closed the blinds in an attempt to conceal their flaw from God and each other. How terrible it must have felt to see such an ugly brand on their once-perfect heart, to see a monstrous dragon crawling around in their previously pure soul, to sense the tree — root, trunk, branches, and all — had gone bad. Their race to conceal shows how little we've changed over the millenniums.

Like Adam, after sinning
we instinctively lower the shades
so nobody can see what we've done
and who we've become.

When God finally confronted them, they didn't say, "You're right. Thanks for pointing out our mistake." No way! They evaded responsibility by pointing a finger at someone else. Adam blamed Eve and Eve blamed the Serpent.

Like Adam and Eve, we all frantically try to cover our sin and all the shameful memories and habits it has produced. Controlled by our flesh, we seek someone or something to blame for who we are and what we've done. Tragically, as long as we succeed in hiding our shame, we remain slaves to the dragon who resides in our soul.

Fortunately, God refused to allow Adam and Eve to stay in hiding. He chased them down and dragged them, along with their guilt and shame, into the light. He exposed what they had been trying so hard to hide. Then, and only then, did they find renewed intimacy with him and with each other.

The Real Enemy

Of course, we know something Adam and Eve didn't. We know they were the key players in a struggle between good and evil, a battle between God and Satan. The only question that mattered was who would win domination over their souls ... good or evil.

Satan loves to whisper in your ear, "If anyone knows what you've done, they'll reject you. Keep it hidden. What they don't know won't hurt you."

Because you believe that lie, his words shackle you to shame — like a prisoner chained to a dead man — and you know, or think you know, that people will avoid you just as they would a decaying body. No wonder you feel unworthy and afraid to let others see what you're really like. No wonder that such shame-driven fear of rejection causes you to place a higher value on hiding than on your friendship with God.

Unfortunately, the situation is worse than you think. It reminds me of the doctor who called a patient and said, "John, I've got bad news and really bad news. Which do you want first?"

"Give me the bad news."

"I got back the results of the tests and you've got two days to live."

"That's horrible," John said. "Wait a minute — what's the really bad news?"

"I was supposed to call you yesterday," the doctor said.

The bad news is that you may be suffering from a form of toxic shame that drives you to hide from God and other people and medicate your pain with sexual immorality. I'll share the really bad news with you in the next chapter.

FOR DISCUSSION

1. How can embarrassment be good for us? How is it different than shame?

2. How is guilt different than shame?

3. Why is shame dangerous to a man's soul?

4. Why does a shameful man not want to look closely at himself?

5. How did God greet Adam and Eve after they sinned? How did that help them?

6. What do you think God does after you sin? How does that help you?

7. What was the real battle Adam and Eve were involved in? What does that mean for the rest of us? Since you're in Christ, who will ultimately win the battle for your soul? How does that knowledge affect you today?

Grab the Grace of God

The really bad news is that behind your obsession with sexual immorality lurks an idol and behind the idol prowls a demon.

It's easy to deny or ignore this truth because we tend to think of an idol as some sort of stone or metal image in the shape of a man, like the fat Buddha. But an idol is anything we trust besides God to meet our deepest needs.

In 1 Corinthians 10:19–20 (NIV) the apostle Paul says, "Do I mean then that a sacrifice offered to an idol is anything, or that an idol is anything? No, but the sacrifices of pagans are offered to demons, not to God, and I do not want you to be participants with demons."

Paul pulled the disguise off the ancient pagan idols and revealed an ugly demon. Those who offered sacrifices to stone images were worshiping the demon behind the idol. This truth is spooky enough to come from a Stephen King novel. But it's not fiction. It's as reliable as God's Word. When a man gives himself to an object of sexual lust, he's embracing the demon behind the object. He's cohabiting with an evil spirit. As I noted earlier, I believe that's one reason why sexual sins exercise such power over a man.

Grabbing the Grace of God

When we refuse to go into the cave, grab our sin — with all its shameful memories and habits — by the ears, and drag it into the light, we suffer a greater tragedy. Jonah said, "Those who cling to worthless idols forfeit the grace that could be theirs" (Jonah 2:8 NIV).

I could live my life and miss out on lots of things that wouldn't make any difference. Things like skydiving, bungee jumping, orbiting the earth, golfing with a president, or attending a Super Bowl. But there's one thing in this life I don't want to miss out on because doing so would mean I wasted my life. How? By wasting countless chances to lay hold of God's grace. More than anything in life I do not want to miss out on the grace of God.

I don't want to be like the kid who slipped his hand into an expensive vase. When he couldn't get it out, he ran screaming to his mother. When she saw her son swinging his arm around like a windmill trying to free his hand from the vase she almost fainted ... not because she feared for her son, but because she feared for the vase.

Never one to panic — she might faint but she'd never panic — the mother found a bottle of liquid detergent and shot some of it over her son's hand. She held the vase and told him, "Pull hard." He grunted and groaned and huffed and puffed and pulled and tugged, but he couldn't dislodge his hand.

The situation looked bleak when, after the boy's hand had only been in the vase ten or so minutes, his father walked through the front door of the house. He quickly assessed the situation, tried unsuccessfully to pull out the hand and announced, "I'll have to cut off his hand."

Upon hearing that proclamation the boy started wailing uncontrollably.

"Funny," the wife said to her husband in a tone that meant, "You're a jerk and you abuse children emotionally."

He had meant it as a joke. "Okay, I won't cut it off," he said. "I'll have to break the vase."

"Maybe you *could* cut it off," the wife whispered in a tone that said, "I can be funny too."

A moment later the dad gently tapped the neck of the vase hoping it would break along the seam. Instead, it shattered into 236,432 razor-sharp slivers.

Initially, the mother felt grave disappointment. Then she saw something that defied all reason and caused her to question the intelligence of her son — who just an hour earlier had seemed like an exceptionally bright and gifted child.

The boy stood with a clinched fist over the table that held the shattered pieces of the vase. "Were you making a fist all the time we were trying to get your hand out of the vase?" she asked.

The tone of her question along with a stern look caused the boy to swell up like a toad. [In that moment the mother thought about the recent media reports of numerous toads in the Altona district of Hamburg that swelled up with gases and exploded, propelling their innards for distances of up to one meter.[1]] She quickly stepped back a couple of feet and watched as tears streamed down her son's face.

"Why didn't you open your hand?" she asked.

The child uncurled his soap-covered fingers revealing a silver coin. He stared at it and blubbered, "I was afraid I'd drop my quarter."

Frankly, I don't believe that story. I mean how could a kid actually be that stupid? I don't think so. Yet, while I don't think a kid could be that stupid, I wouldn't put such idiocy beyond a grown man like you or me. Like that boy, we sacrifice God's grace when we hold on to an object of our lust.

God says, "Let go and you get my grace. Hold on and you'll shatter the power of my grace in your life."

You don't have to forfeit God's grace, however. You can let go of the idol you're holding, but doing so will require more than opening your fingers. First, you must drag everything you're ashamed of out of the cave and into the light.

Then you must let it go. Once you do that, you'll discover that you've also released the object of your sexual obsession and started down the path to sexual purity.

The apostle John spoke of the benefits of living in the light when he said, "If we walk in the light, as he is in the light, we have fellowship with one another, and the blood of Jesus, his Son, purifies us from all sin" (1 John 1:7 NIV). Purity occurs when we bring our sin into the light of God's presence.

Stop Playing Dodgeball

Dragging our shame into the light means we need to stop playing dodgeball with the truth about ourselves. At the turn of the century the game made a comeback. I suspect it's because of the movie by that name that starred Vince Vaughn, Christine Taylor, and Ben Stiller.

As a child I loved playing dodgeball. But I didn't just play the game. I dominated.

At the time all my classmates thought I was destined for the dodgeball hall of fame. The game allowed me to showcase my speed, agility, strength, and guts. The pathetic truth is that the ninth grade was the greatest year of my life ... athletically speaking.

During that one year I reached the zenith of my athletic prowess. I remember buying a football-letter sweater several sizes too large so it would still fit me a year or two later. But I never grew any taller. I didn't get any faster. I've still got that white sweater in my closet, and I remember how it used to hang on me like a potato sack. Every time I look at it I'm saddened by the crushed dreams it represents. If I had just been bigger, faster, stronger, taller, and had a higher pain threshold I could have been an NFL quarterback.

Anyway, at the zenith of my athletic life, I wasn't just *good* at dodgeball, I was great. I was lightning quick and could evade almost any ball thrown. If I couldn't dodge it, I'd catch it and hurl — no *hurl* is the wrong word — I'd *rocket* the ball at an opponent, and he'd be out of the game. Oh, the faded memories of childhood greatness.

While you may have never played the game, or maybe you haven't played it in years, there's another game you may be pretty good at: spiritual dodgeball. I know it sounds corny, but it's the truth. Most guys are expert at evading responsibility and throwing it at someone or something else. By dodging responsibility, we hope to avoid the suffering that occurs when we see and embrace our sinfulness.

In his book *People of the Lie*, M. Scott Peck describes people who are dedicated to maintaining an appearance of moral purity. They're aware of their own evil but are frantically trying to avoid that awareness. He defines an evil person as someone who is "continually engaged in sweeping the evidence of their evil under the rug of their own consciousness."[2]

Tragically, since evil people want to dodge, or disguise, their evil, they're often found involved in churches.[3] Why? Because by cloaking themselves with the robe of religious activity, they can conceal from themselves and others the true nature of their soul.

The two friends I mentioned in the opening story of this book wore all the trappings of spirituality. They had led small groups and served on the board of the church without anybody guessing that they were secretly watching a neighbor from a window of their house. Some men carry out a double life for decades.

Facing Our Dirty Secrets

Of course, as sinners, we're all capable of doing just about anything. The question is, what will we do about our bent toward evil? Will we keep dodging the truth, or will we let it hit us square in the face? If we let it hit us, if we allow the truth to nail us, then we'll have to look at the nasty secrets about our family and ourselves. The secrets our sin uses to create the shame that drives much of our compulsive sexual behavior —

- Secrets about physical and sexual abuse
- Secrets about alcoholism and brutal family fights
- Secrets about other addictions and the grave consequences that flow from them
- Secrets about imperfections you never talk about
- Secrets about your own sexual behavior

Secrets like these are the source of your shame. They are the reason you don't believe anybody would love you if they really knew you. They are the reason you keep others, even those closest to you, at arm's length.

Assume Responsibility

It's important to realize that those secrets aren't excuses. They don't justify our behavior. They're simply the painful truth about our past and present. They're the thoughts and memories that feed our feelings of shame. Not only must we face those secrets, we must identify how and when we've blamed others for our predicament.

Several years ago, while I was doing a live radio interview, a caller said, "I think churches need to do something about the way young women dress." He then went into such detail describing how some of the young women, with an emphasis on the word *young*, dressed at his church that I thought I heard him panting over the phone. With increased agitation and excitement he said, "Why, these girls come into church wearing short skirts and plunging necklines. You can see the cleavage of their breasts. They need to be told to cover up."

After he hung up his phone and listened to his radio, I suspect he was more than a little surprised by my response. I told him, "When the church starts legislating dress, then you can count on the fact that unchurched people will not walk through the door. Modesty is a characteristic of maturity. As a woman grows spiritually, the Spirit of God will prompt her to dress modestly."

After making that opening statement I said, "But, sir, the real problem isn't how the women in your church dress. It's your inability to control where you look. You will never be able to control what women around you wear. But you can control where you choose to look."

By blaming the young women in his church for inappropriate dress he let himself off the hook. We all need to realize that

women who dress suggestively aren't to blame for our destructive sexual behavior

our parents aren't to blame

our wives aren't to blame

pornographers, prostitutes, and dancers aren't to blame

So who's to blame? Look in the mirror. The guy staring back at you is the one responsible for getting you into a mess. That is the simple truth you must embrace. He's the one who chooses to allow his sin, his flesh, and its dragonish appetites to control his thoughts and actions.

And because the man in the mirror is a new man in Christ, a good man indwelt by God's Spirit, he does not have to live that lie.

Three Lists

Take some time right now, or whenever you can find a quiet, private place. With three sheets of paper, write out the following lists:

- *List Number One:* Identify every shameful secret you can think of.
- *List Number Two:* Identify every excuse, justification (something that justifies or makes what you've done okay), and rationalization (false reason for your actions rather than the real reason) you've made for your behavior.
- *List Number Three:* Identify those people you've blamed for your current situation.

Making these lists is crucial. It enables you to identify those memories you've hidden that your old self uses to feed your shame. It enables you to stop allowing your flesh to deceive you into blaming your circumstances and other people for your problems. Once you've made the lists, you're ready for the next step.

Tell God

So far only you've seen your stuff. Now it's time to show it to someone else. I'd encourage you to bring it to God since he already knows about the dragon of what you're like and what you've done.

Nobody illustrates better what you need to do than the Prodigal Son (Luke 15:11–32). If anybody had reason to fear rejection, it was him. Itching to indulge his lustful appetites, he demanded his share of his father's inheritance. What a conversation that must have been.

"Dad, would you give me my inheritance now?"

"You'll get it when I die."

"I want it now."

"Son, you'll get it when I'm gone."

"Yeah but, Dad, you seem healthy and I can't wait that long."

"What's your plan?"

"To get as far away from you as I can so I can do what I want."

"Do you realize what you're saying?"

"Yes. I'm saying I'd rather have my inheritance than you."

So his dad sold off half of his holdings and handed over the money to his son.

That much money made the boy quite popular in the "distant country." What a party life he enjoyed. His house overflowed with friends, beautiful women, wine, and more beautiful women. He bought every fantasy a man could imagine.

Then he ran out of cash and his friends ran out on him. Nothing like finding yourself a long way from home with no friends, no money, and no job. Desperate, he went to work feeding pigs. It's strange how an empty stomach can cause a man to consider getting on his hands and knees and joining the pigs for dinner.

Then he hit the proverbial bottom of the pigsty. From that vantage point, home seemed a lot better, and his dad's food seemed a lot tastier. Then he realized that none of his dad's servants ate with pigs.

A kid's got to be pretty desperate to return home to a father he spat on, but because he came to his senses he realized he belonged at home with his dad. Even if he had to work as a servant, he had to get back to his father. Filled with shame, he headed home. With every step he reviewed another sin he had committed against his dad.

The reason Jesus told that story was to educate the ancient religious leaders about how God views sinners who come home. Sinners like you and me. Men who have committed some serious sexual sins and wonder how God will respond if they turn to him.

God Loves You

What the prodigal didn't know was that his father had kept an eye on the road that led to his home. Day after day he prayed for the return of his son. Day after day he gazed at that road, hoping to see the confident gait of his son walking toward him. You see, when the prodigal left he took with him a part of his dad's heart, and as long as he remained away the father lived with a chunk missing from his heart. And he needed it back.

I think one of the great pains the father of a prodigal lives with is caused by the fear he'll outlive his son. No, it's worse than that. He grieves the death of his son as though he has already died. It's a lingering grief that has the power to slow the passage of time and age its bearer and create a sadness that stays as close as a shadow.

How crazy must a man be to think such a father would love him less because he has sinned? Yet the prodigal thought that and so do most men. Still, the moment the father realized his son, the one he thought dead, was alive and walking toward him, he ran down the road to meet him. Before the son could blurt out his confession the father embraced him and kissed him.

Jesus wants us to know how God feels about people like you and me, people who have turned their backs on him and done stupid and sinful things.

God Accepts You

It's no surprise that the prodigal didn't expect a corner office and company car when he returned. He would have been happy cleaning toilets. But his father did the unexpected. He restored him to a position of honor and influence.

When a man has wasted years of his life it's natural for him to feel remorse. Not just because of the past damage he's done, but because he's sacrificed his future. He's certain God will toss him into the wastebasket. He knows his life will be a story of unrealized potential. After all, how could God possibly use someone with such a sordid past.

Instead of a stiff arm, the prodigal's father gave his son a robe, a ring, and sandals, because he accepted him completely — no holding back. He would retain the honor, authority, and work of a son.

Because I've done more than my share of stupid things, I'm thankful that God uses broken men. Maybe that's why the story of Peter's denial of Jesus inspires me. After informing Peter that he would deny knowing him three times, Jesus said, "I have prayed for you, Simon, that your faith may not fail. And when you have turned back, strengthen your brothers" (Luke 22:32 NIV).

I suspect those words took on a special meaning to Peter when he later felt as useless as a broken bow. He must have found hope in the fact that Jesus not only predicted his denial, but his repentance and future usefulness as well. God loves prodigals like you and me. And he loves to take broken men and make the rest of their life the best of their life.

God Celebrates Your Friendship

What a party! The father prepared a banquet, brought in a band, and invited everyone he knew. Why? Because the son he believed dead had returned home alive.

How different the party scene would have been if the boy had never returned home because he feared his father's rejection. The life of Jesus screams that God accepts sinners and celebrates their friendship.

You know that list I encouraged you to make a few pages back? The one you hope nobody ever sees? The one you think will cause God to frown? Listen, the moment you show it to God, he'll give the signal initiating a celebration in heaven with confetti, streamers, and party whistles. Nothing gives him more pleasure than his friendship with you, and nothing will give him greater joy than for you to drag your shameful thoughts and memories into the light of his presence so he can forgive you, cleanse you, and prepare you for future use.

Accept Yourself as God Does

Of course, the healing of shameful thoughts and memories won't occur overnight. You'll still struggle with the fear of rejection and abandonment. Since you may relapse, thoughts of self-condemnation could overwhelm you. You may say to yourself, "It's no use. I'm too far gone to deal with this" or "There you go again! You've confessed your sin to God and done the same thing all over again. You're no good!"

The next time you hear a voice whispering those thoughts stop and tell yourself, "These thoughts are not coming from God. They're a lie. They describe my old man. They deny my identity as a new man in Christ." Remember, one of Satan's primary roles is to accuse God's people and cripple them with guilt and shame (Revelation 12:10).

After you've said that to yourself you must choose to counteract the lie with truth. You must tell yourself, "God unconditionally loves me. He has made me a new man in Christ. I accept his love and my new identity. I love myself."

Whenever lies about who you are start bouncing around in your head, tell yourself this. If you're alone, say this out loud. Say it often! For years you've probably been telling yourself that you're a terrible person. God is transforming your mind and character, but it will take time for you to embrace your new identity. Yet if you'll diligently talk to yourself this way you'll begin to see yourself differently, and as you see yourself as God does, your thinking and actions will change.

Because we realize most love is conditional, we've studied and practiced making ourselves more lovable. We do all we can to make ourselves look better, smell better, and sound better. We try to wear the trappings of success that tell the world we're worthy of respect and love. You know what I mean — cars, clothes, houses, vacations, offices, and all sorts of toys.

Anyway, it makes sense since we live in an "earn my respect and love" kind of a world, we would try to win God's love. The truth is there's nothing you can do to make yourself more lovable to God. He wouldn't love you more if you were perfect. And he doesn't love you less because you're not. You're loved just as you are. If you refuse to believe you're loved, you're calling God a liar. You're implying you can determine your value better than God can. Only an idiot would imply that. Oh yeah, I've already established that we men are sometimes idiots. So when you fall into such thinking, remind yourself that such thinking is idiotic and untrue.

Jesus wanted us to grasp the reality of God's unconditional love. I'm convinced that's why on the night before he died he prayed that all believers would live in unity to let the world know — and this phrase blows my mind every time I read it — "that you sent me and have *loved them even as you have loved me*" (John 17:23 NIV, italics mine). Did you catch the last phrase? Jesus said he wants us to know that God loves us as much as he loves him. God the Father loves you as much as he loves Jesus. He loves you, his imperfect son, as much as he loves his perfect son.

Saying, "I accept God's love and my new identity," counteracts the lying voice of your sin which fuels your feelings of shame. Each time you repeat that sentence, you're tapping into the love of God. And his love has transformed you and will continue to do so.

Putting Your House in Order

The process of personal change occurs over the course of our lifetime because it takes a lifetime to begin to grasp who we are as new men in Christ. Now that you've dragged your shameful secrets into the light, the next step involves deciding whom you will serve — your lust with its dragonish appetites, or Christ.

FOR DISCUSSION

1. How is sexual sin a form of idolatry? What does Paul say is behind an idol? How does that truth affect you?

2. How do men play spiritual dodgeball? Why do they play it?

3. Do you play that game?

4. What are the secrets in your life you want to keep hidden? Have you ever told anyone about them? How do you think they would respond if you told them?

5. First John 1:9 NIV talks about how God will respond if we bring our sins to him. It says, "If we confess our sins, he is faithful and just and will forgive us our sins and purify us from all unrighteousness." What two things will God do when you confess to him?

6. Bring the three lists you made to God. Confess your sins to him.

7. What is the result of your confession?

8. How does it affect you to know that your heavenly Father loves you, accepts you, and celebrates his friendship with you?

PART THREE

FINDING FREEDOM

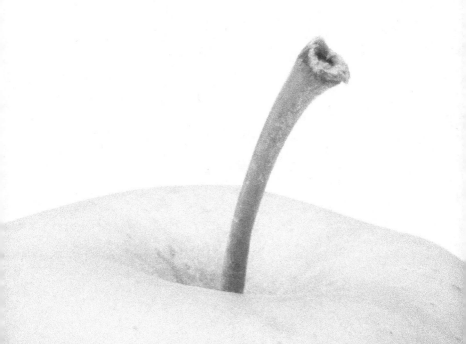

Count the Cost

I used to barefoot water-ski. I thrived on the adrenaline rush of skimming across glass-smooth water at high speeds. I enjoyed using my heels to create six-foot-high rooster tails made of water. I savored the challenge of performing tricks like a deep-water start or crossing the wake or skiing on one foot or managing a tumble turn. All of those things I liked about barefooting. I did not like falling face-first against a plate of placid water while going forty miles an hour. That I did not like.

One day a friend approached me and said, "Could you teach me to ski barefoot?"

Since he already knew how to slalom I said, "No problem."

"Really?"

"Yeah, provided you're willing to repeatedly fall face-first while racing over the water at forty miles per hour."

"I can handle that," he said.

I smiled. This would be interesting. I considered testing his resolve with a couple of sharp slaps across the cheeks. Instead I said, "The key word you may have missed in my condition was the word *repeatedly*."

The first face-plant he experienced painted his face a bright red, cleaned out his sinuses, made his eyes bulge, and stole his enthusiasm. As I brought the boat around he sputtered that he would give it one more try.

The second face-plant ripped off his hair, tore off his wet-suit, and moved his nose to the back of his head. Or so it seemed to him.

"Maybe you can give it a try later on," I said in an effort to restore his dignity.

"Yeah, later."

Of course, he never tried again. I knew he wouldn't. But over the years I've taught a lot of guys to barefoot. They're the ones who won't give up because of multiple face-plants.

The funny thing is that the guys who stick with it aren't more athletic or courageous or less prone to feel pain than the guys who give up. The single difference in these men is commitment. They've made up their minds, before they step onto the water, that they'll ski barefoot, and eventually they do. The other guys like the idea of barefoot skiing but only if learning is quick and easy and painless.

When I've taught a friend to ski barefoot, I always try to make it clear up front how bad it hurts to eat the lake at high speeds. Since I don't want them to fail, I encourage them to count the cost before trying it.

In a similar way, I want you to consider the cost of moral purity.

"I want it," you say.

"But it will hurt to change the way you think and live."

"Right."

"You'll be giving up something that gives you pleasure."

"Right."

"It will require a total reforging of the way you see your-self and how you act."

"Right again."

"You'll fall on your face."

"I know."

"You'll fall more than once."

"I don't care. I want purity."

Is that pretty much the way we'd talk if you and I were sitting across from one another at Starbucks — or some other coffee shop? If so, then before you make the commitment, I want you to count the cost. Doing so is crucial for your long-term success.

Count the Cost

When I looked up the definition of the word *gravity*, I found it a bit more complicated than I imagined. *Gravity*: "The natural force of attraction exerted by a celestial body, such as Earth, upon objects at or near its surface, tending to draw them toward the center of the body."[1] I thought I'd read, "Gravity is what makes things fall." Or "Gravity is the force behind the saying, 'What goes up must come down.'"

While you've heard of gravity I suspect you've never heard of what psychologist and author Abraham Twerski calls the "law of human gravity." In his book *Addictive Thinking* he writes, "A person gravitates from a condition that appears to be one of greater distress to a condition that appears to be one of lesser distress, and never in the reverse direction."[2]

Simply put, Twerski contends that people always choose the course of action that produces the least pain. In other words, a desire to avoid pain exerts a gravitational force on a man's soul that pulls him in the direction of lesser pain and more pleasure.

When I first read Twerski's law of human gravity, I assumed it meant that the only people who break free of compulsions and addictions are those whose lives are in total disarray, those who have lost everything. But that's not necessarily true. Any man can find freedom from a sexual sin, but he will only do so if the pain of continuing in his behavior is greater than the pain of stopping. The pain of continuing can either be produced by losing everything he values or by experiencing less significant losses and contemplating the loss of everything else.

My friends who learned to ski barefoot endured physical pain because they convinced themselves that the pain of failure was greater than the pain of falling. They endured the shock of slapping the water with their face at high speed because they imagined the pleasure of success.

Yet once they had that vision of success, they still had to take a step of faith. They had to commit themselves and place one foot into the water and a moment later lift the other foot off the ski and put it into the water. They took that step knowing full well they were only a blink away from greeting the water with their face.

Nowadays ski instructors use a boom bar to help people learn to ski barefoot. A boom bar is a metal bar that extends over the side of a boat. The skier holds onto the bar, skims across the water on his backside, and when the boat reaches the right speed, he swings his feet around and skis barefoot. Boom bars diminish the frequency of falls, but nobody learns to ski barefoot without experiencing pain.

Similarly, there are things you can do to diminish the likelihood you'll fall back into sexual sins (we'll examine these in later chapters). But you'll never be pure without a willingness to undergo periods of discomfort. Since that's the case, you have to commit yourself to God and a process that will promote purity.

You can either wait until, like the Prodigal Son, you've reached the bottom of the pigsty. Or you can exercise wisdom by seeking to understand the consequences of your sexual sins if you don't find freedom. How can you do that? Again — it won't happen if you kick back and wait for the insight to land on your shoulder. Such understanding doesn't come to us anymore than a butterfly would. But you can gain it if you'll take some time and follow my next coaching tip.

Make a List

I remember reading a book by a well-known pastor, Jay Dennis, about achieving and maintaining sexual purity. In the opening pages of the book he describes his thoughts and feelings after cheating on his wife. I hadn't expected such an uninhibited confession. In fact, I was shocked that he had committed adultery at all.

I sat up and read intently as he described driving his car to his favorite spot ... a place where he routinely met with God ... a spot where he led a men's discipleship group. As tears streamed down his face he contemplated telling his wife. She had been with him through the worst and best of times. She would ask a single question: "Why?"

Then he thought about telling his son and his church. How would his act affect his son's view of him and of God? How would it affect those he led and those he had led to Christ?

Then came the biggest surprise of all. He said none of that happened because he hadn't had an affair. He explained that he had written that story years before to remind himself of the high price he'd pay if he cheated on his wife.[3]

That story blew my mind. I went from emotional agony to unexpected joy as I imagined his living through such torment and then realizing none of it had happened. Not to him or me.

Here's the deal — as men our memories may not recall an important date or appointment, but we seldom forget the face and body of a hot woman we've seen in the past. We can remember in high definition every feature of her face and form. But imagining the consequences of sexual sins evades our grasp like so much smoke. That's why it helps to write out a list. It sears on our memory what would happen if we did the unthinkable.

With that in mind, take a few minutes and make a list of the consequences of continuing your harmful sexual behavior. Or maybe you're not currently heading down that track. If that's the case, then follow the pastor's example and make a list anyway. Your list should include consequences you've already suffered and a future worst-case scenario. Use the list below and add to it if necessary.

Painful Consequences
If I Follow the Path of Sexual Sins

1. To my marriage:

2. To my family:

3. To my job:

4. To my health:

5. To my reputation:

6. To my self-image:

7. To my finances:

8. To my future:

Painful Consequences If I Stop

1. Boredom

2. Enduring emotional pain instead of deadening it with sex

3. Enduring an intense craving for destructive sexual experiences

4. _____

5. _____

Hopefully, making these lists and seeing the pain of continuing in your sin is greater than the pain of stopping. These lists are aimed at helping you say, "Enough is enough. I've had it. I want freedom, even if I have to endure pain to find it."

Once you've made these two lists, make a third one, which describes the benefits of moral purity.

Benefits of Purity

1. To my relationship with God:

2. To my wife:

3. To my children:

4. To my health:

5. To my reputation:

6. To my close friends:

7. To my self-image:

8. To my finances:

9. To my future:

Take some time to complete these lists. Use the suggested consequences and benefits as starting points. Add others that may apply to you.

As you examine these lists, it will become clear which choice brings the greatest benefits.

Unfortunately, when it comes to sexual sin, we men aren't always logical. We act like the man who was digging ditches during a hot summer day in Texas. After he had worked for several hours, a buddy said, "Why is it we're out here break-ing our backs for minimum wage, while the president of the company makes a six-figure salary for practicing his putting in an air-conditioned office?"

"I'm going to find out," the man said, throwing down his shovel. He marched toward the office building that housed the company's executive suites. In a few minutes he was standing before the company president. "Why do you make so much money for doing hardly any work, while I dig ditches and make so little?"

The company president flashed a friendly smile and said, "Come over here, and I'll show you." He then held out his hand in front of a brick wall and said, "Hit my hand with your fist."

The worker hauled off and swung at the president's hand with all his might. Just as his fist was about to make con-tact, the president moved his hand, and the ditchdigger's fist slammed into the wall. As he yelled in pain, the president said, "That's why I'm the president and you're a ditchdigger."

The worker returned to his buddy, who asked, "What did he tell you?"

"I'll show you," the worker said as he lifted his hand in front of his face. "Hit my hand as hard as you can."

It's tough to imagine anybody being that ... hmm, it seems the word *stupid* keeps showing up, yet we men can be just that illogical when it comes to lust. We'll do things that create unimaginable pain for ourselves and for those we love. I'm challenging you to resist the urge to be illogical. Look at the price of sexual sins and the benefits of purity and make a commitment to stop your destructive sexual behavior. Or if you're not involved in sexual sins, make a commitment to avoid them.

Once you make that commitment, you're ready for the next one. Turn the page to find out what it is.

FOR DISCUSSION

1. Review the two lists of consequences for continuing or stopping your destructive sexual behavior. As you go over the lists, try to visualize the consequences of each decision. Ask God to enable you to be especially clear in seeing the consequences of continued sin.

2. Write a one-page story describing what it would be like for you to have to tell your wife, children, and friends. If you're meeting with a group, share what you've written with them.

3. How does contemplating such horrible consequences affect you now?

4. Now review the list that states the benefits of purity. Share that list with your group. Ask God to help you see the blessings associated with living a sexually pure life.

5. Thank God that in his strength you're able to move forward as a new man in Christ.

Choose Your Master

I'm twenty-one years old and at a friend's apartment. We're smoking dope. I've been dating Cindy, my future bride, for three months. When we're together I'm Mr. Straight Christian Guy. I'm moving in the right direction spiritually, but I enjoy getting high.

Chelsea takes a drag on the joint and holds the smoke in her lungs. Her long blonde hair hangs over each shoulder. The whites of her eyes are bloodshot. After ten or so seconds she slowly blows out the smoke that smells like a song from the Grateful Dead. She looks at me and asks, "Who knows you better, Bill, Cindy or me?"

The question seems odd. I see Chelsea every couple of weeks for a few hours. She hardly knows me. Cindy and I had spent countless hours together since we'd met. "Cindy," I say.

Chelsea responds to my answer like she expects it. "Cindy doesn't know this side of you. Does she?"

Her comment stuns me. I stare at her for five or maybe ten seconds.

"See what I mean?" she asks.

I see what she means. I'm living two lives.

An hour passes. My head clears. I climb into my red Austin Healey 3000 and head home. The top is down and the cool spring air blows through my hair. But it's God's Spirit that's blowing through my heart. Around midnight I drive south on Lamar Boulevard and cross the bridge over Town Lake in Austin. Halfway across the bridge I see a fork in the road of my life. On the left is a life of hedonism and materialism — a life that's halfhearted in its commitment to God. To the right runs a road of purity — a life wholly devoted to God.

I feel God tugging at my soul. I must decide. Which will it be? I can't continue to have it both ways. One or the other. Tears stream down my cheeks. In that moment I dedicate myself to pursue God for the rest of my life. I would not smoke dope again. I would not sleep with a woman until she was my wife. Before that moment I knew Christ as my Savior. With that decision he became my Lord.

In the previous chapter we saw the importance of making a commitment to a life of purity. In this one we'll examine the value of committing your life to God.

I don't think it's a two-step process. It's not as if we make one commitment and then the other. They occur simultaneously. When a trapeze flyer is about to jump, he's making two commitments. He's committing to release the trapeze and grab the catcher. Without both commitments he'll fall. The same is true of us. We must let go of our sin and turn to God. In this chapter we'll discover how, now that we've let go of the trapeze, we can grab the hands of God.

Ending Isolation

Because lust is a spiritual problem, it isolates us from who we are in Christ — our true self — from God and from people. The longer sin runs unchecked — with all its lustful appetites — the more spiritually isolated we become. When fully in control of our lives, lust prevents us from connecting with God or other people. Our lust seeks to smother the new man in us — our true personality — and destroy our spiritual life.

In the early stages of a sexual sin, the object of our lust (the idol and the demon behind it) seems to nurture life and bring fulfillment to our inner self. The rush of pornography or an affair exhilarates and makes a man feel alive. But as a sexual sin progresses, the nurturing proves to be a mirage. That's why as lust consumes us, a spiritual withering occurs.

> *For freedom and healing to take place,*
> *we must reconnect ourselves to God*
> *and cultivate our spiritual life —*
> *the new man, the good man we've become*
> *through our identity with Christ.*

Our willingness to grab hold of an idol in the form of a sexual object shows our need for God. It reveals the hunger in our soul for something outside ourselves. Saint Augustine wrote about this hunger centuries ago: "Our hearts were made for you, O Lord, and they are restless until they find their rest in you."

God wants to give you this rest. He wants you to experience union with him so you can grow spiritually. That's why Paul exhorts us to offer our bodies to God as living sacrifices (Romans 12:1).

A Logical Choice

For years it seemed like every time I saw someone dedicate themselves to God it happened in an emotionally charged setting. After a powerful and moving sermon the pastor would challenge people to come forward and commit their lives to Christ. And people would go forward. Occasionally, a friend of mine would accept the challenge.

At youth camps, after a week of intense spiritual input, kids would be exhorted to devote themselves to God, and many of them, in tears, would do just that.

It didn't take long for me to draw two conclusions. First, God can and does use our emotions to draw us to himself. Two, there is a potential pitfall with emotionally driven spiritual decisions. Namely, when the emotions that prompted the decision pass, so may the commitment. It reminds me of someone who makes an impulse buy and then later experiences buyer's remorse.

I'm thankful for the intense religious experiences I've had. Some of them have led to a deeper commitment to God. The experience I had that night in Austin while driving over the bridge was pretty emotional. But many of the long-lasting commitments I've made to God resulted from thinking through exactly what God wanted me to do and then deciding, by God's grace, to do it.

I think that's the approach the apostle Paul had to commitment. When he urged the Romans to present their bodies as living sacrifices to God, he said that such an act was a "reasonable" act of service (Romans 12:1 AMPLIFIED). In the original language, *reasonable* meant "based on logic."

Before asking them to make that commitment, Paul began his exhortation (NIV): "Therefore, I urge you, brothers, in view of God's mercy ..." The apostle used the word *therefore* because he wanted his readers to consider everything he had said to them in the previous eleven chapters. In those chapters he explains that God's mercy provides us with forgiveness, acceptance, freedom from lust, a wonderful future, and the power for a victorious life. And of course, God's mercy has identified us with Christ so that we're new men in him.

In light of all God has done for us through Christ, and in light of all he will do for us in Christ, doesn't it make sense that we should devote ourselves completely to him? Does pornography deserve our devotion? Does a prostitute? An illicit affair? Of course not! God alone deserves our devotion, and he alone can exercise his mercy on our lives in such a way that he prompts us to give ourselves to him in love. Did you catch the meaning of that last phrase? It's God's mercy that has already changed us, and it's his mercy that will bring us to the place of total devotion to him.

Of course, our lustful appetites will resist the mercy of God. They'll whisper lies in our ears that can become fortified barriers to keep away God's goodness. It's crucial you know about these barriers so you can allow God's mercy to get past them.

BARRIER ONE: "I've Got to Clean Up My Act"

"I'm not ready to devote myself to God," you say.

"Why not?"

"Because I'm hooked on porn."

"So?"

"Well, I can't commit myself to God until I've stopped visiting porn sites on the Internet."

"Listen, God doesn't ask you to fix yourself and then turn to him. He wants you to come to him broken so he can heal you."

It's a profound reality that God loves you just as you are. It's his power that will change you, not your own. Jesus compared our friendship with him to that of a branch and vine — we're the branches and he's the vine (John 15:1 – 8). The job of the branch is to abide in the vine and bear fruit. It's the responsibility of the vine to produce the fruit. Similarly, living a sexually pure life is the fruit of a friendship with God, not the prerequisite.

A person becomes a Christian by trusting Christ to forgive his sins and give him eternal life. Christ died on a cross to pay the penalty for our sins and rose from the dead to assure us of eternal life. The only thing left for us to do is trust in him. Our faith unleashes his infinite power to save.

Just as faith connects us to God, it's also the key to a growing friendship with him. As followers of Christ, we must commit ourselves to God and trust him to change us. Our faith taps into his unlimited strength (Ephesians 1:15–23). That means you don't have to get your act together before devoting yourself to God. In fact, if that's what you're waiting for, you'll never devote yourself to God because you'll never completely clean up your life.

BARRIER TWO: "I Committed Myself to God Before and It Didn't Work"

This line reminds me of a friend who went on a diet and later complained that it didn't work for him.

"Why not?" I asked.

"Because when I ate less food I got hungry."

"Did you expect the diet to take away your hunger?"

"Well, no. But I didn't expect to be *that* hungry."

"Maybe if you try it again, and stick with it long enough, your hunger will eventually subside."

"Nah," he said, "it didn't work for me."

Of course, committing yourself to God will no more take away your lustful appetites than a diet will remove a man's hunger for food. It's understandable that a guy would think, or at least hope, that when he committed himself to God, the Lord would remove his lustful desires. When the lust remains he might conclude that God had let him down and spiritual dedication doesn't work. The truth is, God doesn't remove our lust — he gives us the guidelines and power we need to control it.

While God has made us new men in Christ, we still sometimes allow our sinful appetites to control our lives. Growth occurs as we understand our new identity in Christ and live consistent with our new life. But just as a growing child will fall when learning to walk so will we. In fact, grown men occasionally stumble. Commitment to God works because it allows us to tap into his grace which changes the way we think and act.

BARRIER THREE: "I've Committed Myself to God in the Past and Don't Need to Do It Again"

Like wedding vows, our initial act of devotion to God occurs only once. But like wedding vows, it can be renewed — and should be renewed if you've turned your back on Christ and embraced a life of sexual immorality.

Over the years I've performed wedding ceremonies for married couples who are renewing their vows. In some cases they do so to break formally with an incident of infidelity. They can't remarry each other, since they're already married. But they can renew their commitment to one another.

Sometimes men need to do that with God. They need to renew their act of commitment as a formal way to tell God — and themselves — that he is their Lord and Master.

BARRIER FOUR: "I'm Unworthy"

"I've done some pretty bad things. No way do I deserve God's love," you say.

"You feel unworthy and unable to change. Right?"

"Yeah, that's right."

Well you need to know that you're *not* worthy of God's love, and you *can't* change yourself. If you'd like some biblical proof check out Romans 3:9–20; 7:23–24, and James 2:10. But you're just like everyone else. In fact the Bible is filled with stories of men whose struggle with sin proved their unworthiness and humanity. Consider:

Jacob lied.

Moses murdered.

Samson slept with a hooker.

David committed adultery and murder.

Peter denied knowing Jesus.

Don't kid yourself — even the most admired men in the Bible blew it.

> *The Christian life isn't about being perfect*
> *and deserving God's favor.*
> *It's about taking a few steps,*
> *stumbling, getting back up,*
> *and taking a few more steps.*

Hopefully, over time we won't stumble as often or fall as hard. But one thing is sure: no matter how pure we may be, we'll never deserve God's favor. And we'll never be able to change ourselves. Since that's the case, we should devote ourselves to the One who loves us anyway and has the power to change us.

Give Yourself to God

If you'd like to dedicate yourself to God, I encourage you to do so now. Perhaps it would help for you to imagine yourself as a prodigal son returning to your Father. As you approach, you see him standing on the front porch of a great house. Right away you recognize him. The moment you've anticipated is here. To help deal with your nervousness, you rehearse what you'll say.

When you're about as close as a football field, he realizes it's you. Immediately he steps down from the porch and begins jogging toward you. As he gets closer, you can hear your heart beating. Suddenly he's there in front of you — smiling. Instantly he throws his arms around you.

Now it's time for you to tell your heavenly Father what you've done wrong. Express your sorrow. Tell him you're ready to commit your life to him. Let him know you're doing so because you want to serve him rather than your lust. You want to live according to the new man he has made you, not the old man who's driven by lust.

By doing this, you're placing your life in his hands. Unlike the animal sacrifices offered by the ancient Jews, you're presenting yourself to God as a living sacrifice. You're giving him your body for his use. You're saying, "Here Lord, I give you my mind, and eyes, and ears, and hands, and feet. I give to you all of my sexual thoughts and activities. They all belong to you and are devoted to serving you."

Such an act is not only reasonable, it's deeply spiritual. You're to live your life for him and allow him to live his life through you.

A Crisis of Faith

Once you dedicate yourself to God, two things will happen. First, you'll be made aware of changes that must take place in your life. On August 21, 1971, Cindy and I stood before one another, exchanged marriage vows, and said, "I do." Later we moved into a small apartment on Cedar Street in Austin, Texas.

It wasn't long before we realized we would both have to change if our marriage was going to work. I'd have to show my love by driving slower, being more sensitive, listening better, writing her poetry, going for long walks with her, watching less TV, driving slower, giving up some sporting activities, driving slower, sleeping less, and, oh yeah, driving slower.

That's a list of eight specific things I could do to strengthen our marriage. I had a list for Cindy too: show up naked and bring food.

A similar thing happens after we commit ourselves to Christ. God shows us areas of our lives that must change. While it's true that God accepts us just as we are, it's also true that he never leaves us that way. The Lord will show you thoughts and actions that must change if you're going to be sexually pure. He will point out things that can't be present in your life if you're going to draw near to him.

But a second thing will happen. As you contemplate these changes, you'll experience a crisis of faith. You'll come face-to-face with whether you believe in God or are enamored with the idea of faith in God.

During the time you've been indulging your lust, you've been trusting yourself to meet your needs for intimacy and pleasure. You've been relying on an object, a person, or an experience (and the demon behind it) to satisfy your longings. It will be painful to let go. Doing so will be like hitting the water face-first while traveling forty miles per hour. It will hurt. Everything in you will plead to satisfy your lust once more.

At that point in time, you'll face a crisis of belief. Will you trust God to meet your needs or will you meet them yourself? Will you obey God or not? There's no way around the crisis of faith.

Throughout the Bible, whenever God called a man to himself, the man had to decide whether or not he believed God could be trusted to take care of him. With Abraham, that meant leaving his homeland and traveling to an unknown country. He did that because he believed God would take care of him. Later he offered up Isaac as a sacrifice because he believed God would raise him from the dead (Hebrews 11:17–19).

God has called you to dedicate yourself completely to him. By doing so, you're saying you believe God will protect and provide for you. That act of commitment will bring about changes in the way you think and act, and it will lead to a moment in which you'll be forced to decide: "Can God meet my needs, or will I trust sex to meet them?" You'll face that question every time you're tempted to think or look or act in a way that gratifies your sexual appetite outside of God's will.

Obviously, you're reading this book because you want to be pure. Many men dedicate themselves to God and then fall back into sin because they don't have a clear understanding of their new identity and the changes God wants them to make so they can keep their lust under control. As a man who wants to be pure, you need to know the adaptations God wants from you. In the remainder of this book, we'll examine some biblical guidelines that God's Spirit will use to reshape the way you think and live.

You Can Do It!

It's 5:30 a.m. and I roll out of bed. I'm seventeen and living with my parents on Timberline Drive in Rollingwood Estates, just outside of Austin. I climb into a pair of cutoffs, slip on a T-shirt, slide my feet into a pair of sandals and walk out to the car — a black and white '56 Pontiac ... a junker that shakes like a jackhammer when it approaches 75 miles per hour, dislodging dust from the upholstery and headliner and filling the interior of the car with floating dust particles. Twenty minutes later I drive into the parking lot of the pier where the ski boat is docked. My buddy is waiting.

We step into the boat and I slip the key into the ignition. I turn the key, the 150-hp engine gurgles, and the smell of gas fumes waft through the air. The early morning lake looks as smooth as glass, and like a mirror it reflects trees on the far shore.

In the middle of the lake I kill the engine and explain to my friend what he has to do to barefoot ski. "Put your left foot in the water and lean back so far you think you'll fall. Okay?"

"Okay," he says.

I feel his excitement and fear. "And then lean back further," I say. "If you fall backward, it won't hurt. If you fall on your face that's another story."

But of course that happened almost a lifetime ago. Or so it seems. Right now we're not talking about skiing. But as I write these words I feel a similar sense of excitement. You're about to embark on an endeavor that will involve some risk and pain. But it also promises great rewards. I'm nervous as you step out of the boat and commit yourself to Christ, and I'm eager for you to read the rest of the book because you know as well as I do that devotion without direction is a blueprint for defeat. In the rest of the book I'll provide you with a strategy that will enable you to live pure for the rest of your life ... or at least one day at a time.

I'm confident that, by God's grace, you can do it.

FOR DISCUSSION

1. Romans 12:1–2 (NIV) says,

   Therefore, I urge you, brothers, in view of God's mercy, to offer your bodies as living sacrifices, holy and pleasing to God — this is your spiritual act of worship. Do not conform any longer to the pattern of this world, but be transformed by the renewing of your mind. Then you will be able to test and approve what God's will is — his good, pleasing and perfect will.

   Read these verses several times. Have several men read them out loud. How does Paul describe the act of commitment in verse one? What will characterize a man who has made that commitment?

2. Which of the barriers to commitment discussed in this chapter have you had the hardest time getting past? Have you gotten past them yet? If so, how do you do it?

3. Are you at a place where you're ready to make Christ your master? If not, why not? Ask God to help remove any barrier that's hindering your commitment to him. If you're ready then you could do so now by offering a prayer like this: "Father, I recognize your mercy has brought me to faith in Christ. Your mercy has forgiven me and made me a new man in Christ. And now, in response to your mercy, I devote myself to you. I place all I am and hope to be before you. I ask that you'll transform my mind and make my life one that proves how very good your will is. I pray this in Christ's name. Amen."

4. If you've committed, or recommitted, your life to Christ, tell a friend. It will help you and encourage him.

Discover the New You

On July 8, 1947, an alien spacecraft crashed outside of Roswell, New Mexico. While the crash of the UFO is common knowledge, few know that before dying the lone surviving alien managed to safely store a single pod in a rift near the crash site.

For years everyone always told me, "You're strange," or, "You're really different," or, "You're from another planet." They would even joke about the fact that I grew up in Roswell.

Of course I always took such comments as friendly banter until the day I flew to Albuquerque and rented a car and drove two hundred miles southeast to the crash site outside of Roswell. Once at the site I realized it was an excellent place for an alien craft to crash — in the middle of nowhere. Except for the sighting by a rancher nobody would have known.

Anyway, as I stood in the middle of a barren field, surrounded by rocks and tumbleweeds, a beam of light enveloped me. Before I could identify the source of the beam I passed out.

When I woke up under a Mini-Cooper-sized tumbleweed, I held a book in my hands. It couldn't have been more than two hundred pages long and weighed less than a pound. It carried the title *Understanding Your Alien Identity.* I thought the book looked irrelevant since I was born and raised in New Mexico and could prove my US citizenship. Then I remembered my wife saying, "I think that UFO must have deposited an egg that hatched two years later. That would explain your ... umm ... existence."

Curious I opened the book and thumbed through its pages. If I was indeed an alien I would have hoped for a revelation about my identity that would take me to a place like Superman's Fortress of Solitude that's 130 miles due south of the geographic north pole. That's a cool place with huge crystals and where Superman's father, Jor-El, appeared to him in the form of a hologram.

All I had was a book that, fortunately for me, was written in English and not some alien script. Anyway, I've spent years studying the book to understand my unique alien powers so I could utilize them for the benefit of truth, justice, and the American Way (sadly, Superman's motto has been changed from "the American Way" to the politically correct, "All that Stuff").

The truth is I'm an alien. But my alien identity wasn't derived from an extraterrestrial who left an egg on a hillside in New Mexico. It was derived from God when he gave me his Spirit and made me a new creation in Christ (2 Corinthians 5:17). Peter told his readers that they were "aliens and strangers" (1 Peter 2:11 NIV) and that they have an "inheritance" that is kept for them in heaven (1 Peter 1:4). Paul told the Philippians, " ... our citizenship is in heaven" (Philippians 3:20 NIV).

It's a spiritual reality that if you know Christ,
you're an alien who is visiting this world.
You're a stranger here.
You're truly a new man,
a good man, in Christ.

The key to moral and sexual purity is found in your new identity. Ultimately, when any of us fall into sexual sin it's because we've allowed our flesh to steal our identity so that we think and act consistently with its sinful passions. We must recognize when this happens and choose to act in a manner that reflects our new life in Christ.

If the truth of this chapter sinks into your mind, it has the power to radically change you for the better. You see, an encounter with Jesus Christ transforms the genetic stuff of your spirit. If you'll invest some time and study the book that explains your new identity, inheritance, and new power over your flesh, you'll see yourself from God's perspective. When that happens, you'll live like the new man, the good man, you are in Christ.

The point is this: when you trusted Christ, you became a new man, and it will take time for you to understand your new identity. The more you realize who you are the more you'll live like a son of God — an alien in this world.

As I noted in the previous chapter, once you devote yourself to Christ, God will point out ways you need to change — and no change is more important than how you see yourself.

You're Unconditionally Accepted

God's unconditional acceptance is tough to comprehend. You may wonder how he can overlook all the terrible things you've done. Actually, he doesn't overlook them. On the contrary — Jesus died on a cross to pay for them.

When I first heard this message, I was greatly relieved. While growing up, my family seldom attended church, and when we did go, I felt as out of place as a Hell's Angel at a police convention.

I divided people into two categories: good guys and bad guys. I definitely fit into the bad-guy category, but I did believe in God and wondered how I could know him. My religious friends tried to help me out. Some told me I had to go to church. Others said I had to stop swearing, cheating, stealing, and getting into fights. They might just as well have told me to change the color of my eyes. I could no more stop my bad behavior than fish could walk on dry land.

But I tried. I attended church and found it boring. I remember looking around and wondering how anybody could sit through such dull sermons. I figured maybe the pastor sold his sermons at drug stores to help people who suffered from insomnia. Ultimately, I concluded something was wrong with *me*.

I tried to stop swearing. In fact, one year my friend, Ben Smith, and I gave up swearing for Lent.

"What's Lent?" I asked.

"It's the forty days leading up to Easter," he said.

"So why do we give up something for that?"

"It's got to do with identifying with Christ fasting in the wilderness for forty days. We do it to make God happy."

"What should we give up?" I asked.

"Cussing," Ben said.

So Ben and I went to school the next Monday morning determined not to swear for forty days. I know the purity of my lips impressed all my friends. Until then I cussed so much that by eliminating those words from my vocabulary I didn't have much to say.

Everything was going well until my third-period PE class. We were playing field hockey and I recall running full speed toward the ball and hitting it with my stick. At the same time Virgil Lewis was racing toward the ball from the opposite direction. Instead of hitting the ball, he swung his stick full force and hit my left shin. In less than ten seconds every foul word I knew spewed from my mouth. To make matters worse, I attacked Virgil and busted his nose with my fist.

In that moment, I realized what I had known all along I'd never be good enough to please God. So you can understand why I was relieved, as a freshman in college, to discover God only wanted me to trust in him. He simply wanted me to rely on his Son for forgiveness. Once I understood that Jesus paid for my sins through his death and offered me eternal life through his resurrection, I believed (Romans 4:5; 10:9–10; Ephesians 2:8–9). I trusted Christ as my Savior.

What amazed me the most were the immediate changes that occurred in my life. Habits I had struggled with for years were shed like soiled and tattered garments. Seriously, I even stopped swearing. Well, I'd occasionally swear, but not like I had before. Some of the changes were so profound I hoped my lust was a problem of the past.

Four Steps to Freedom

Of course, I was wrong. When my lust stirred from its slumber after I had trusted Christ, it scared me. That's when I found, in the writings of Paul, some insights that altered how I handled my lustful appetites. And in the next chapter I'll share four specific steps that Paul gives us to assure our freedom from lust.

FOR DISCUSSION

1. Because sexual purity flows from your new identity in Christ, it's important that you know him. With that in mind, have you come to a place in your life where if you died you know for certain you'd go to heaven? If you got there and God asked, "Why should I let you in?" what would you say?

2. If you answered that last question by saying anything other than "I believe Christ died for my sins and was raised from the dead, and I've trusted him alone for forgiveness and eternal life," you may not know Christ. Neither good works nor religious rituals will get us into heaven.

3. Ephesians 2:8–9 (NIV) says, "For it is by grace you have been saved, through faith — and this not from yourselves, it is the gift of God — not by works, so that no one can boast." According to these verses, what is the one thing a man must do to be saved from his sin and its consequences? Would you like to trust Christ as your Savior now? If so, you could do so with a prayer like this, "Father, I thank you that you love me. I admit that I've sinned against you. I believe that Jesus Christ died for my sins. I believe he died in my place and was raised from the dead. Right now I'm trusting him alone for forgiveness and eternal life. Amen."

4. If you trusted Christ as your Savior, 1 John 5:11–13 (NIV) says, "And this is the testimony: God has given us eternal life, and this life is in his Son. He who has the Son has life; he who does not have the Son of God does not have life. I write these things to you who believe in the name of the Son of God so that you may know that you have eternal life." According to these verses, can a man know for sure he has eternal life? If so, how? Do you now have that assurance? If so, tell a friend.

Four Steps
to Freedom

"Let me get this straight," John said. "You're telling me God has forgiven all my sins. Right?"

"Right."

"And no matter what I do in the future it's forgiven because Christ was punished for my past and future sins. Right?"

"Right again."

"I think there's a major problem with what you're saying."

"What's that?"

"Well, if my future sins are already forgiven, what's to keep me from doing bad stuff?"

"What keeps a butterfly from crawling like a caterpillar?"

"Huh?"

"You heard me. What keeps a butterfly from crawling like a caterpillar?"

"Well, he's been changed. He's no longer a caterpillar. He's a butterfly and so he can't do what he used to do. Plus, why crawl when you can fly?"

"You've answered your question."

"How's that?"

"When you believed in Christ, God changed you from the inside out. He made you a new creation ... a new man. You're not a caterpillar anymore, you're a butterfly. Why crawl in the dirt when you can fly?"

I've had countless conversations like that one. Thinking men who understand the complete forgiveness God offers through Christ want to know what will bridle their sin. If the fear of punishment is removed, what's to keep a man from indulging every lustful fantasy?

When Paul wrote his letter to the church in Rome, he knew some would say his message of complete salvation by faith promotes lawlessness. His critics would argue that if God freely forgives all who believe in Christ, nothing prevents people from satisfying their lower appetites. Paul said such thinking fails to understand a spiritual reality.

> *God has fundamentally*
> *changed a man's nature.*
> *He has turned caterpillars*
> *into butterflies.*

All who believe in Christ have been identified with him in his death, burial, and resurrection. This spiritual reality forms the basis of our new identity. Everything that's true of Christ (apart from his nontransferable divine attributes like omniscience, omnipresence, and omnipotence) is true of us. We're in Christ, like a page in a book. What's true of the book is true of the page. That truth forms the first step you must take toward freedom from sin.

STEP ONE: **Know Who You Are in Christ**

As I mentioned earlier, Jesus compared our friendship with him to that of a branch in a vine. When Jesus prayed on the night prior to his crucifixion, he said, "I pray also for those who will believe in me through their message, that all of them may be one, Father, just as you are in me and I am in you. May they also be in us" (John 17:20–21 NIV). While the Lord was talking about unity among believers, he was also recognizing our position in him.

Paul told the Galatians, "I have been crucified with Christ and I no longer live, but Christ lives in me" (Galatians 2:20 NIV). The old Paul, all he was before he met Christ, died on the cross. Now he was a new person — united with Jesus in his resurrection life.

I used to watch *Star Trek — Deep Space Nine.* In fact, I'm not sure I missed an episode of the science-fiction series. One of my favorite characters was Lieutenant Jadzia Dax, an attractive and brilliant young woman who looked like any other woman. Well, she looked like any other woman except for a narrow banner of paisley-like markings that ran across the side of her face and body. Those markings identified her as a member of Trill, a unique race in which some people play host to another race that lives within them and is joined to them.

Jadzia was the host to a three-hundred-year-old symbiot, Curzon Dax. Without losing her own identity or personality, Jadzia benefited from the experience and knowledge of Curzon Dax. The two blended together in such a way that they were truly one totally new person.

In a sense, that's what happened when we become followers of Christ. The Spirit of the living God comes to dwell within us. In a mysterious way, God's Spirit intertwines with ours and we become a new person (2 Corinthians 5:17). That means that on the planet Earth there are two unique and different species: sons of Adam and sons of God.

Because we are actually new people, a whole new creation, it would be inconsistent for us to live as we used to live. It's not that we've adopted a new religious philosophy that teaches us to try to live better lives. We've been transformed. In Christ our new man has freedom from the power of sin and its lustful appetites (Romans 6:1–14). Paul wrote, "We died to sin; how can we live in it any longer?" (Romans 6:2). It's important to note that Paul didn't say that our sin, or lustful appetites, died. He said we died.

Since none of us have died physically, Paul had to be referring to another kind of death — a spiritual death. He taught that all who believe in Christ are spiritually identified with him in his death, burial, and resurrection. God somehow pulled us through space and time and placed us into Jesus during his crucifixion and resurrection. It's not that we lose our individuality. Instead we are indwelt by Christ. Everything that's true of him is true of us.

This concept has life-changing power, because it describes a spiritual reality. It describes a new you.

Consider for a minute the implications of this truth. Does sin have power over Christ? Of course not! Since that's the case, it also has no power over you. Paul wants us to realize it's inconsistent for us to allow our lustful appetites to control our lives, since we've died and been raised with Christ. We're new men, identified with Christ. The risen Lord of the universe actually lives in us!

At the home where I grew up in Roswell we had crab apple trees growing in our back yard. One day I pulled an apple from a tree and bit into it. Bad decision! I expected something sweet and got a mouthful of bitter. I immediately spat out the apple and expressed my disdain with a flurry of foul words.

I'm thankful to David Needham, who used the crab apple tree as a vivid illustration of what happens when a man becomes a Christian. Having tasted the bitter fruit I understand why he used it to represent our essential nature before we trusted Christ. The apostle Paul noted in Ephesians 2:3 (NASB), "Among them we too all formerly lived in the lusts of our flesh, indulging the desires of the flesh and of the mind, and were by nature children of wrath, even as the rest."

Like a crab apple tree that produces sour apples that are destined for destruction, so our evil nature produced sinful deeds that resulted in misery and death.

But suppose that one day my dad, tired of the sour fruit of the crab apple trees, made a diagonal cut across the trunk of one of the trees. And then he took a fresh green section of stem, cut with a matching diagonal slice from a different tree, and spliced it onto what was left of the trunk. Next he wrapped and sealed the slice and supported the new stem with a brace. Before leaving he attached a tag to one of the new branches that said, "Golden Delicious Apple."

In the months that followed, buds would have appeared above the splice line. Eventually they would blossom and produce not crab apples but golden delicious apples. No longer would it be a crab apple tree, nor would it be a crab apple/ golden delicious tree. It would be a golden delicious apple tree. That would be its true identity.

But the tree would still have some identity issues. Why? Because below the graft, sucker shoots would grow. And if they weren't cut off, they would produce crab apples. But those sucker shoots and their fruit would be usurpers deserving one thing: removal.

My dad would have to work diligently because the buds below the graft would want to grow. If he failed to remove them they would so dominate the tree that its true identity would scarcely be seen surrounded by the wild growth from below the graft.

But even if that happened, my dad would not have changed the tag. Why? Because the essential nature of the tree remained a golden delicious apple tree. The sucker shoots had to go because they no longer represented the true identity of the tree.[1]

The story illustrates what Paul is teaching us in Romans 6. The moment you trusted Christ, your old self was cut off, crucified. What you had been by nature, "children of wrath," you are no more. At this moment you're a new man, a golden delicious apple tree. You truly are a new man!

But as you know, the root and base of the old trunk still remain in you. It has not changed at all. The old crab apple within you tries to grow sucker shoots that will produce crab apples. But no matter how many crab apples — sexual sins — appear in your life, by nature you're a new man.

You've been released from the power of your sinful lusts. Twice in the first six verses of that chapter, Paul uses the word *know*. The first step in grasping your new identity involves knowledge. You're a new man because you've been joined with Christ, and your old man's lustful appetites have no more power over you than it has over him. He is the golden delicious apple tree that's been grafted into you, changing your identity.

STEP TWO: **Believe You Live with Christ**

Because you've been dominated by your flesh and its lust for so long, you may not *feel* its power has been broken. You may *feel* like a crab apple tree. You may not *feel* like a new man in Christ — a golden delicious apple tree. Regardless of how you feel, you need to know that Christ has shattered the power of the old man with its sinful appetites. You no longer have to give in to your lustful desires. The sucker shoots from the base of the tree do not need to grow in your life and define your identity.

Knowing that the power of sin has been broken enables us to live above the downward pull of lust. Believing we "will also live with him" (Romans 6:8) enables us to move forward with our lives. It's our belief, our faith, in Christ that unleashes his unlimited power to produce golden delicious apples in our lives.

Jesus has called you to a friendship with himself. All of his power and victory now belong to you. This truth is so real, Paul exhorts believers to "count yourselves dead to sin but alive to God in Christ Jesus" (Romans 6:11 NIV).

You may not think you have enough faith. But you do.

> *You exercise enough faith every day to unleash the power of Christ through your new man.*

I suspect you have a car sitting in your garage, driveway, or carport. Under the hood of that car rests an engine. Almost every day you climb into the car, insert the key in the ignition, and start the engine.

That activity involves faith in the car, key, and motor. There may be days when the car is dirty and doesn't look as if it would go anywhere. On other occasions you may not feel like driving it anywhere. But regardless of how the car looks or how you feel, if the automobile is in operating order and you turn the ignition key, the engine will start. The car will take you where you want to go.

Christ's power over sin won't do you any good unless you utilize it. You do that by knowing that all that's true of him is true of you and by trusting him to live his life through you.

STEP THREE: Give Yourself to God

While you know how to start a car engine, you may be less sure how to utilize Christ's power. Paul gives us specific guidance when he tells us to give the members of our body to God as "instruments of righteousness" (Romans 6:13 NIV).

The moment you're tempted to read pornography, surf the Net for erotic images, flirt with a coworker, or visit a strip joint, you're making a decision based on how you view yourself. If you see yourself as a slave to sin, unable to say no to your sinful desires — the crab tree that's in the lower part of the tree — you'll probably obey the commands of the crab tree and produce crab apples — lustful thoughts and actions.

If you see yourself as free from the power of sin, you'll present yourself as God's slave and walk away from the temptation. You'll produce golden delicious apples because you're a golden delicious apple tree.

How do you exercise faith in your car? You get in it, start the engine, and drive away. In other words, your faith is demonstrated by your actions. Similarly, you exercise faith in Christ by looking to him when you're tempted, and trusting him for the power you need to obey.

The next time your lust whispers in your ear, turn away from it and look to Christ. Don't struggle with your lust yourself. Don't resist it by saying, "I can't listen to it." Instead turn to God and say, "Father, thank you for delivering me from my lustful appetites. Thank you for giving me the power of Jesus.

Right now I'm trusting in him to enable me to live according to my true identity and experience victory over sin."

Let's say you're working out in the gym and an attractive girl walks by wearing an outfit that compliments, or exposes, her most attractive features. You glance at her and it feels good. You hear your lust pleading with you to keep looking at her beauty or to inconspicuously follow her around. If you say to yourself, "I won't look," chances are you'll keep looking.

Instead say, "Father, I thank you that I'm a new man ... a good man in Christ. Right now I'm trusting in the power of Jesus to enable me to look away."

That strategy works whether it's a hot girl at the gym, an attractive and flirtatious coworker, an image on your computer, or a woman you see walking down the street. If you try to fight against your lust in your own power, you'll lose. It's too strong. Instead allow Christ to fight for you.

When I was in the ninth grade, Ron Kompton, a fellow student, despised me. Ron looked like a giant. He was a man among boys. He stood six feet three inches tall and weighed 230 pounds. I was only five feet nine inches tall and weighed 130 pounds. Ron's fist was almost as large as my head.

One night at a party Ron arrived late. When he discovered I was there, he hunted me down. In a few minutes he was calling me names and shoving me around. Like an idiot, I allowed him to coax me into the front yard, where he said he was going to kill me.

I did everything short of falling on my knees and crying like a baby to talk Ron out of beating me to a pulp — and I would have done that if I had thought it would save me.

We were standing in the yard surrounded by about thirty kids, who were urging us to get it on. Suddenly a car screeched to a halt at the curb. A moment later the door slammed and someone yelled, "Kompton!"

I recognized the voice. It was my best friend, Mike Temple. Mike was the only guy in town bigger and meaner than Ron Kompton. Before graduating from high school, Mike made the all-state football team twice as a fullback. Later he played college ball for Oklahoma State. He was a tough kid and loved to fight.

Mike quickly pushed his way through the crowd, walked up to Kompton, shoved him back, and said, "Kompton, if you're going to touch Perkins, you'll have to go through me!"

I felt a surge of courage and stepped up to Ron. "That's right, Kompton," I said, "and don't you ever forget it!"

Ron started whimpering about how he didn't realize Mike and I were buddies. He assured my friend he'd never bother me again.

I like that story, because it illustrates how Jesus fights for me. I don't need to suffer any more humiliating defeats.

By faith we believe that Christ has delivered us from sin and lust. Our union with him is the source of our self-control. We must believe that we're identified with him and that he is the source of our victory. We need to accept his victory in our minds and spirits.

STEP FOUR: Don't Give Lust a Foothold

There's more to victory over sexual lust than knowing we're identified with Christ and have victory in him. The battle against lust isn't won by understanding alone. Nor is it assured because we have access to the power of Christ. We have to be diligent in our refusal to give lust a foothold in our life.

Paul wrote, "When you offer yourselves to someone to obey him as slaves, you are slaves to the one whom you obey —

whether you are slaves to sin, which leads to death, or to obedience, which leads to righteousness" (Romans 6:16 NIV).

It's easy to believe that lie that says, "One little sin won't hurt. One look at the inserts in the newspaper won't do any damage — they're hardly erotic. One glance at an Internet porn site won't hurt — what harm is there in a quick glance? One flirtatious conversation won't matter — we're just friends kidding around."

Paul's message is clear: "No way, José! One tiny sin leads to enslavement." Ultimately, you determine by your choices who will be your master. If you give your lust a small snack — an extra glance or flirtatious smile, it will demand your life. It will become your master. On the other hand, if you give yourself to Christ, he will be your Master.

Three Elements of Victory

Before we move on, I'd like to summarize what we've learned in this chapter. There are three important elements that will help the new you experience victory over sexual lust. It would be helpful for you to read these aloud until you've learned them. Once you have them memorized, frequently repeat them aloud.

Perspective

I'm a new person. I see my sexual lust differently. I'm united with Christ, and the power of my sin and its lustful appetites has been broken. I don't have to obey its commands any longer.

The next time I'm tempted to commit the tiniest of sexual sins, I'm going to thank God he delivered me from that. I'm going to reflect on the fact that I'm in Christ and all that's true of him is true of me. Jesus wouldn't give in to the temptations I face, and in him I won't either.

Presence

I'm not alone in my struggles. There is One within me who knows my weakness and accepts me as I am — Jesus Christ, my Savior. The next time I feel alone, I'm going to remember that Christ is with me. Rather than looking to a sexual experience to meet my need for intimacy, I'm going to look to Christ.

Power

I have the power of the risen Christ living within me. I don't need to argue or fight with my lustful appetites. I don't need to vow to resist their enticements. When I'm tempted, I can turn to Christ and trust him to infuse me with his resurrection power.

Perspective, presence, and power are three elements that make up the new you. But living free requires another element. In the next chapter I'll give you a strategy aimed at helping you live free for the rest of your life. And I believe what you'll read may be the most useful information in this book.

FOR DISCUSSION

1. What kind of new identity did you receive when you trusted Christ? How does the illustration of the golden delicious apple tree explain your new identity? What will the lower part of the tree try to do? Do the sucker shoots define your true identity in Christ? What does?

2. What steps can you take to enable you to experience victory over your lustful appetites? Review exactly what you'll say to yourself the next time the good man in you is tempted to lust after a woman.

3. Why is it dangerous to give lust a foothold in your life? How can you prevent this from happening?

4. What are the three spiritual elements of victory over sexual lust? How can each one aid you?

Guard Your Thoughts

The phone on the credenza behind my desk rings. I pick it up and my secretary tells me that my three-o'clock appointment is here. I check my calendar ... I've penned in the names Jay and Julie Johnson. Hmmm ... their names alliterate. I wonder if they'll name their kids John, Jason, Jane, and Janet Johnson.

I open the door and they walk in and take a seat next to one another on the tan couch that backs up to the wall across from my desk. I sit in the brown accent chair that's to the side of the couch.

I feel a bit awkward because Julie is one of the most beautiful women I've ever laid eyes on. Her blonde hair is cut short, just below her ears. Her flawless skin is tanned and highlights pale blue eyes. Her legs, or what I can see of them, are long and slender.

I look at Jay and wonder, *How did he get her?*

I ask general questions and discover how he got her. Jay's intelligent, witty, and doing well in business.

Finally, I address their problem. "What's the biggest issue you're struggling with?"

They look at each other. "We never have sex," Julie says.

Jay is uncomfortable with her declaration. She's close to tears.

"Can we talk alone?" Jay asks. "Just for a minute."

"Is that okay with you?" I ask Julie.

She nods her head and walks through the door.

"What's up?" I ask Jay.

"I didn't want to say this in front of Julie, but frankly I find it easier to masturbate than have sex with Julie. It's just less hassle."

It's a good thing he can't read my mind. I'm wondering how any man would consider it a hassle to have sex with a woman as gorgeous as Julie.

I assume a nonjudgmental expression and tone. "Does Julie know you're taking care of yourself?"

"No, I'd be embarrassed to tell her."

We chat for a few more minutes, and then Julie reenters the room. I wonder how hurt and lonely she must feel.

We talk for an hour and then they leave. I look forward to each session. We meet several more times, and then one day I get an unexpected phone call from Julie. "We can't come in today," she says. "I was hoping you could come by the house."

"Is Jay there?"

"No. He had to leave town … a last-minute decision by his boss. He'll be back tomorrow. I hoped the two of us could meet together. Alone."

My heart races and I feel a warm glow rush through my body. I make a decision. "Julie, I'm not going to see you or Jay again. I'll call Jay and give him the name of a therapist. I think some of your issues require a more experienced counselor than me."

I hang up the phone and press my face against my desk.

I never see Julie or Jay again. As I reflect on that experience that occurred years ago I'm reminded anew that temptation hits us when we least expect it. I certainly didn't see that one coming my way.

Some temptations, like the one with Julie, take the form of flesh-and-blood women. Others take the shape of a two-dimensional image on a computer monitor or television screen. For the man who struggles with the temptation to sleep around on his wife, the lowering of societal sexual values intensifies his battle. Why? Because more women are willing to engage in behavior that used to be considered wrong.

In regards to digital temptation, it's gotten much worse in recent years. Consider the following statistics:

- At $12 billion per year, the revenues of the sex and porn industry in the US are bigger than the NFL, NBA, and Major League Baseball combined. Worldwide porn sales are reported to be $57 billion. To put this in perspective, Microsoft, who sells the operating system used on most of the computers in the world (in addition to other software) reported sales of $36.8 billion in 2004.[1]

- 33 percent of clergy admitted to having visited a sexually explicit website. Of those who had visited a porn site, 53 percent had visited such sites "a few times" in the past year, and 18 percent visit sexually explicit sites between a couple of times a month and more than once a week.[2]

- 47 percent of families said pornography is a problem in their home.[3]

If you're a man living in the United States, you can't escape sexual temptation — unless you're in a coma and someone is reading this book to you. Eroticism is everywhere. What men used to drive across town to find in a sleazy theater with windows painted black is now offered in the privacy and comfort of their home. And all of this is done in an environment in which we're told it's healthy to indulge our sexual appetites — all of them, in any way we want.

Wouldn't it be great if you could utter a prayer and find yourself surrounded by an impenetrable force field, a defense system that would prevent any impure sensual images from entering your eyes? While such a system doesn't exist, that doesn't mean we can't defend ourselves from temptation. We can. But it will require developing a personal defense system that will guard your purity, a system that will enable you to identify and avoid the dangerous situations offered by our sex-obsessed society. And it will mean deciding in advance how you'll respond when tempted.

Temptation Always Follows the Same Path

Fortunately, the cycle from thought to sin always follows the same path. I call it the "temptation cycle" and every time you sin sexually you follow it. That's why this chapter, and the next one, are so crucial. Within their pages you'll develop an understanding of the temptation cycle and develop a strategy to avoid it.

We've already seen that we all have lustful appetites that are obsessed with one thing: sexual gratification at any cost. Once a man's lust is aroused, all sense of right and wrong goes down the drain. Men will sacrifice everything for a moment of sexual pleasure. Just ask some of the guys caught on Dateline's show *To Catch a Predator.* Businessmen, teachers, coaches, and even pastors all enter the home of a decoy pretending to be a fourteen-year-old girl with whom they've chatted online. They're there with the intention of having sex with that underage girl. In some instances they confess actually watching previous broadcasts of the show. What would drive men to do something so crazy? The answer is simple: unbridled sexual lust.

Our vows of commitment to God mean nothing to our mind once it's controlled by lust. Why? Because a man controlled by his flesh is incapable of obeying God. Paul said as much when he wrote, "The mind set on the flesh is hostile toward God; for it does not subject itself to the law of God, for it is not even able to do so, and those who are in the flesh cannot please God" (Romans 8:7–8 NASB).

In the previous chapter we examined the new identity and nature that we have because we're in Christ (2 Corinthians 5:17). We saw that as long as we're trusting Christ to live within us, the power of our sinful appetites is broken — the crab tree is under control, it's sucker shoots cut off, and we're acting like golden delicious apple trees. The problem is, a battle for domination is being waged within us. Our sinful, lustful appetites — the crab apple trunk and roots — struggle against our new nature to control our will and direct our body. Once we give our lustful appetites a beachhead, they'll take over our life.

Preventing that from happening involves recognizing that our lust always assaults our mind in the same way. Fortunately for us, James, the half-brother of Jesus, has provided us with the Enemy's battle plan. Once we understand that plan, we can form a strategy for defeating it.

Earlier I noted the four stages of the "addictive" cycle:

Now we'll look at the "temptation cycle" through the eyes of James. The stages of temptation he mentions are:

These four stages parallel those used today by psychologists to describe the "addictive" cycle. While James wrote two thousand years ago, he clearly defined the cycle we struggle with today. He urged his readers to be aware of the cycle so they could avoid it.

STAGE ONE: **Preoccupation/Enticement**

James wrote, "Each one is tempted when, by his own evil desire, he is dragged away and enticed" (James 1:14 NIV). In the original language, the words for "dragged away" and "enticed" are fishing terms. They speak of a fish being drawn out of its hiding place and attracted by a tempting lure.

So how does a fish respond to temptation?

He moves out of his place of safety.

He swims around the lure.

He convinces himself there's no danger.

He persuades himself he won't get caught.

He tells himself he can take the bait and avoid the hook.

All right, fish can't think, but if they could, that's what they'd be thinking. It certainly describes how men think. Satan or one of his cohorts drops a sensual image into our line of vision. They may use an insert ad in the newspaper, the image on a billboard, an enticing address on the Internet, a sensual scene on television, or a flirtatious coworker. Because these evil spirits have the power to enhance an object so it has a supernatural appeal, the object of our desire takes on an added beauty.

In a moment our lustful desire whispers, "Looks good, doesn't she? There's no harm in thinking about how good she looks. What you would enjoy doing with her."

With little resistance, we listen to and believe the lies of our lust. We convince ourselves that we can mentally play with the bait and not get hooked. We become blind to the danger of the hook and the hand holding the rod.

Because preoccupation involves our mind only, it's easy to minimize the harm it causes. And so we fantasize about past images we've seen on the Internet. We daydream about a girl we had sex with in the past. We mentally undress the hot babe we saw at the gym.

This is the stage of the cycle in which you must take aggressive action. You need to catch yourself daydreaming about porn, strip clubs, past affairs — or whatever else arouses your lust. If you find yourself fantasizing, switch mental gears. Unless you avoid the temptation cycle here you'll move on to the next stage. Once you get there physical sin is unavoidable.

When Satan tempted Jesus in the wilderness, the Lord didn't give his offers a second thought, even though the temptations addressed areas of intense need. For instance, Jesus hadn't eaten in forty days when Satan urged him to turn stones into bread. Jesus could have reasoned, "Why not? After all, hunger is a legitimate human need, and I have the power to make bread from stones."

The Lord could have considered the suggestion of his enemy. But if you read the story in Matthew 4, you'll notice there is no gap between Satan's temptation and the Lord's reply. Jesus immediately quoted Scripture and rebuffed Satan's attack. He never allowed his mind to play with the temptation.

Such a response demands mental alertness. Peter urged us to "prepare your minds for action; be self-controlled; set your hope fully on the grace to be given you when Jesus Christ is revealed. As obedient children, do not conform to the evil desires you had when you lived in ignorance" (1 Peter 1:13–14 NIV).

An Action Plan for Preoccupation

Cutting off temptation at the enticement stage demands preparation, self-control, and a focus on Christ. How can you do that? Two things will help fortify your mind.

FIRST: **Meditate on Bible Verses**

What you say to yourself at the moment
of temptation is crucial if you're going to disengage
your flesh and trust in Christ for his victory.

As I noted in the previous chapter, don't tell yourself, "I can't think about this. I won't think about this." The moment you think like that, you're actually arousing your flesh. You're focusing on what you shouldn't think rather than on what you should think.

If someone told me never to visualize white elephants and I repeated to myself, "I won't think about white elephants, I won't think about white elephants," what am I doing? I'm thinking about white elephants.

If I tell myself, "I won't think about the girl at work, I won't think about the girl at work," what am I doing? I'm thinking about the girl at work. I'm actually feeding my sexual lust and not the new man in me.

Instead I'm learning to tell myself at the moment I'm tempted, "Thank you, Lord, for saving me from that. Right now I trust you to live your life through me. I trust your Word to purify my mind."

Once I've said that prayer, I choose to fill my mind with passages from the Bible rather than erotic images. Like Jesus, we must use Scripture to expose the lie of a temptation. I've found that memorizing large sections of the Bible gives me a safe mental focus when I'm tempted. By the time I review a paragraph or two, my spirit, my new man, the good man in me, is strengthened and my mind cleared.

The reason this works so well is because God uses the Bible to expose the danger of the bait. To the fish, a lure looks like the real thing. It gives the illusion of real food. Similarly, the object of our lust gives the illusion of intimacy. It promises us pleasure while filling the emptiness in our hearts. Meditating on the truth of Scripture helps us see the illusion for what it is. (In chapter 13 I provided you with some helpful verses.)

There's another reason why meditating on Scripture helps disrupt the cycle. Our minds can only think about one thing at a time. As long as you're mentally reviewing Bible verses, your mind is distracted from the tempting thought or action and your spirit is strengthened.

SECOND: **If You're Married, Think about Your Wife**

Focusing your mind on your wife will strengthen the new man in you. If your wife has lost some of her youthful beauty, then think of her when she possessed beauty. In Proverbs 5:18–19 (NASB), Solomon said this:

> *Let your fountain be blessed,*
> *and rejoice in the wife of your youth.*
> *As a loving hind and a graceful doe,*
> *let her breasts satisfy you at all times;*
> *Be exhilarated always with her love.*

Even when her breasts have begun to sag with age, a man is to rejoice in the wife of his youth. He's to be satisfied with her breasts. By mentally rejoicing in your wife, you'll focus your sexual energies on her. Not someone else.

Of course, if you've been feeding your lust with impure images, it will plead with you to go back to those mental pictures.

It's impossible to stress enough the importance of keeping your mind pure. Jesus said "But I tell you that anyone who looks at a woman lustfully has already committed adultery with her in his heart" (Matthew 5:28 NIV). I don't think

Jesus meant that thinking about committing adultery is as bad as the act. Rather, I believe he meant that the man who thinks about it often enough will carry out the act when given the opportunity. I think one reason I quickly turned down Julie Johnson's invitation is because, while I enjoyed her beauty, I never fantacized about her in any way.

> *In Luke 6:45 (NIV) Jesus said,*
> *"The good man brings good things out*
> *of the good stored up in his heart,*
> *and the evil man brings evil things out*
> *of the evil stored up in his heart."*

The Lord made it clear that good actions flow from good thoughts and evil actions flow from evil thoughts.

I think you'll be surprised at how fast God will cleanse your mind if you'll meditate on his Word and your wife (if you're married). We always remember what we review, and if you'll stop reviewing the impure erotic images and sexual experiences of your past, in time the memories will fade.

While meditating on Scripture and your wife will help you deal with preoccupation, you may be strumming your fingers right now thinking, *I've tried this. It doesn't work.*

If that's what's going on in your mind, I understand. In fact, if all you do is purify your mind I would guess that you'll likely fall back into sexual sins. I don't mean to minimize the importance of focusing your thoughts on what's good. You can't live a pure life without pure thoughts. But if you didn't need something else then I don't think James would have described the next stage of the temptation cycle.

In the next chapter you'll understand that stage and develop a plan to avoid it.

FOR DISCUSSION

1. How have the cultural values of our country changed in the last twenty years? How has this affected you?

2. Why do your vows of commitment mean nothing once your mind is controlled by lust?

3. What are the four stages of the "addictive/temptation" cycle?

4. Why is it easy for us to minimize the danger of preoccupation (enticement)?

5. Why must you take aggressive action in the preoccupation stage?

6. What specific action will you take in this stage in the future?

7. Exactly what will you say when tempted? Compare that with the short prayer on page 176.

Break the Temptation Cycle

"Bill, I've got some really good news," Cindy said. "We're going to have a baby!"

Much to my surprise, I felt a surge of excitement. You may wonder why that would surprise me. Actually, the answer takes me back to a traumatic experience I had an as an eight-year-old. One day my oldest sister, Wanda, brought home her newborn baby. "Do you want to hold him?" she asked.

"Sure," I said.

She started to hand me the child and then hesitated. "You've got to be sure and hold his head securely," she told me. "His neck muscles haven't developed yet, and if you don't support his head it could fall to one side breaking his neck and killing or paralyzing him."

"Oh," I said.

Again she started to hand him to me and again she hesitated. "And you need to be careful not to push your fingers into the top of his head. His skull bones haven't grown together yet, and if you push on that part of his head your fingers could jab into his brain killing him. Or maybe he wouldn't be able to talk or something like that."

"Do you still want to hold him?" she asked.

"Sure," I said.

Wanda handed me her son, and I felt like a contortionist as I twisted my hand to support his head. Had she not mentioned the thing about the top of his head I never would have thought about it. But curious as to how soft his head might be, I used the tip of my fingers to push softly on the crown of his head. It seemed pretty hard to me but I wasn't going to chance it by pushing harder.

I was enjoying the moment when suddenly a geyser of cottage cheese–type stuff mixed with milk gushed out of his mouth and all over my white T-shirt. No sooner had that happened than he erupted at the other end. Disgusted, I held him out to my sister, "Here, you take him."

Ever since that experience I've avoided holding infants. I thought they were cute, in a wrinkled-prune sort of a way, but just didn't care to be around them that much. It's not easy to get over such a traumatic experience.

So when Cindy told me she was expecting a child you can see why my excitement surprised me.

Without wasting time we made a list of things we'd need: crib, drapes, rocker, diapers, changing table, night-light. We were so poor in those days that poor people helped support us. What we didn't receive as hand-me-downs or at baby showers we picked up at garage sales.

For nine months we focused on getting ready for the addition to our family. For nine months we prayed and played and painted and shopped and read and talked. Every thought focused on one thing: the birth of our baby.

We even took a class in natural childbirth. I liked my role. I would stand beside Cindy and pant like a dog. The idea was that if she focused her attention on my breathing and panted in sync with me, it would distract her and diminish the pain of childbirth. Surprisingly, it worked. I felt no pain. Unfortunately, Cindy wasn't so lucky when at two in the morning on July 5, 1976, we raced to the hospital. We had hoped for a natural birth, but after hours of painful labor — painful for her, not me — the doctor concluded the child would have to be delivered by caesarean section.

I find it interesting that when James searched for an illustration of the temptation cycle he decided to use the birth of a child. After describing the enticement stage of the cycle, James changed imagery. No longer did he use the terminology of a fisherman. Instead he spoke of the birth process. He wrote, "After desire has conceived, it gives birth to sin" (James 1:15 NIV).

At this stage we're beginning to give life to our thoughts. The seed of the act has been planted in our minds and is growing. In fact, once the process reaches this stage, the act is as irreversible as the birth of a child once a woman has conceived.

Like a couple getting ready for the day of birth, we focus all our attention on the imminent delivery of the sinful act. We're excited about what will soon take place. Of course, unlike an expectant parent, we don't buy a crib and other baby toys and parenting tools. But there are things we do to prepare for the birth. Psychologists call them rituals. These are the activities we perform before acting out sexually. They express and fuel our sexual excitement. And once we begin to ritualize, we will commit the sinful act.

What makes rituals so insidious is that, like a newly conceived child, they start out so small. It took years for me to figure out that the initial ritual for me was looking at the ad inserts in the morning paper. The pictures of models in swimsuits or underwear seemed harmless enough. It certainly wasn't porn.

But just as a fetus grows, so do rituals. Once I allowed my flesh to feed its lustful passions with a visual nibble from the newspaper ads, it would want more. Soon the sucker shoots from the crab tree would be thriving, and I'd check out the images on some of the DVD covers at Blockbuster. It might take weeks or even a month or two, but as my conscience got progressively harder the rituals would degenerate, and I'd end up checking out girls on the Web in thongs — still dressed, but barely. Then I'd slip over the edge and look at images that were clearly pornographic.

If your struggle is with flesh-and-blood women, not digital images, then the progression would be different, but it ends up with you committing a sexual sin. Maybe your initial ritual would involve flirting with a cute coworker. Next, you'd ask her out to lunch. From there the relationship would progress until the two of you were in bed together.

Stage Two: **Ritualization / Conception**

Nothing is more important
if you want freedom from sexual lust
than identifying the rituals that precede
an episode of acting out.

Some of the rituals men have mentioned to me include

- Surfing the Internet
- Checking out magazines in a book store
- Using your eyes to feast on attractive women
- Driving by a strip club
- Reading personal ads
- Browsing in a video store
- Calling a former girlfriend

- Television channel surfing
- Cruising in a red-light district
- Calling 900 numbers just for information
- Asking a female acquaintance out to lunch
- Oh yeah, checking out ad inserts in the newspaper

Each of us has rituals. Breaking the temptation cycle demands you identify and get rid of every ritual in your life. If even one survives, no matter how seemingly innocent, it will lead to a sexual sin. Take a few minutes and review the list above. On a sheet of paper, write out any of your own additional rituals that aren't on the list.

Once you've got the list, determine exactly what steps you'll take to ruthlessly get rid of every ritual. Next, write out your plan on the page under the ritual.

I mentioned in the previous chapter how nice it would be if we could pray and instantly be surrounded by a force field that would protect our eyes form sensual images. While no such force field exists we can protect ourselves.

Jesus told us to ask God to "lead us not into temptation" (Matthew 6:13 NIV). The Lord didn't mean that unless we asked him not to do so, God would tempt us. God cannot sin nor could he tempt anyone to sin. Instead, we should continually ask God to lead us away from temptation. In essence, we should pray, "Father, never give me the opportunity to sin when I have the desire, or the desire to sin when I have the opportunity." Why? Because when the opportunity and desire to sin intersect, most men will make a bad choice.

While we may not always be able to control our desires, we can usually control our environment. We can eliminate opportunities to sin. We can remove sexual rituals from our life so that when our lust craves a sexual outlet, none is to be found.

We can also avoid those situations that are mined with temptation. It's crucial that we make such choices during times when we're strong.

*In essence, when we're strong
we must make decisions to protect ourselves
from times of weakness.*

I know a man who removed cable television from his home. As a further precaution, he refused to watch television after 10:00 p.m. unless his wife was present.

Another friend who travels extensively refuses to turn on the television in his room. By never turning on the TV, he avoids the ritual of channel surfing.

One man who used to sleep with prostitutes told me he takes an inconvenient route to work to keep from driving through a red-light district.

I've got a friend who said the path to a woman's bed always starts with him checking out attractive women everywhere he looks. He obsesses with looking for and looking at women. In fact, he gets so obsessed that it carries over to his computer. He said he's got to guard his eyes and not let them gaze at lovely women in the course of the day.

Several years ago I signed up with Covenant Eyes, a company that sells a software program that keeps a non-erasable history of everyplace I've been on the Internet. It then identifies any questionable sites and emails the list to an accountability partner. I've discovered I'm as safe on the Internet without accountability as a peg-legged man in a forest fire.

Some guys make up their minds before going to the gym to work out that they won't check out the hot babes. I choose to work out at a time of the day when they're not there.

I know men who are players who must avoid flirting with women. They love the hunt and know that once they start flirting, they've got a knack for getting women into bed. So they keep their work relationships with women on a purely professional basis. In social settings, they're friendly but not flirtatious.

These are examples of the kinds of aggressive steps that we must take to contain our lust.

As you make your list and prepare to break your rituals, expect your lustful appetites to resist — especially if you've been acting out sexually.

Your lust may not appear as a fire-breathing dragon that's destroying your life. It may seem as harmless as a kitten. It will plead with you to keep one ritual — your favorite. It will promise never to ask for more. It will try to convince you that such actions aren't necessary. It will whisper to you that:

"It won't hurt to check out the babes at work."

"You don't need accountability on the Internet."

"There's nothing wrong with a little playful flirting."

"There's no need to look away from the gyrating girls in the beer commercials."

You must anticipate the pleadings of your lust and refuse to allow them to dictate your plan of action. Make the list of rituals that feed your lust and ruthlessly get rid of them. If you don't, the next stage will inevitably occur.

STAGE THREE: Acting Out / Birth

Birth naturally follows conception. The act that has been dreamed about and planned will be carried out. The tantalizing bait will be tasted. If we don't break the cycle at the enticement or conception stages, it's unlikely we'll be able to prevent ourselves from acting out. It's as a friend of mine frequently says: "Once you put your foot on the slippery slope, you're certain to fall." And once we fall, the outcome is truly painful.

STAGE FOUR: Shame / Death

The birth of our first son was more than amazing. After they rolled Cindy into the operating room for her caesarean, I waited near the nurse's station. The waiting area consisted of four chairs on each side of a small table that rested in the middle of the rectangular area. Since it was the day after the Fourth of July, 1976, the magazines on the table all carried headlines about our nation's upcoming bicentennial celebration.

I had been waiting only fifteen or twenty minutes when the speaker that sat on top of the counter of the nurse's station turned on. I could hear a baby crying in the background as a nurse said, "Mr. Perkins, you're the father of an eight-pound, eleven-and-a-half-ounce son."

Words cannot express the exhilaration I felt at that moment. I had no idea the birth of a son would affect me so profoundly.

James wants his readers to know that sin promises such joy. But it never delivers. The baby is always stillborn. I've had friends who lost a young child. There is no greater heartache for a parent than the death of a child. The despair is made worse because it follows months of preparation and dreams and hopes of joy. Instead of holding a bundle of life in their hands, the parents hold a lifeless corpse.

I once had a man approach me after I had spoken on this topic. "Bill do you mean that my baby died because I committed a sexual sin?"

After expressing sympathy for his horrible loss I assured him, "That's not what James was saying. He didn't mean that our sins will cause us to lose a child. He meant when sin is born the baby is always dead. Sin doesn't bring life but death."

During the times of preoccupation and ritualization we anticipate the pleasure our sinful act will deliver. Like an expectant parent, we prepare for the birth of the deed. But when we've carried out the act, after the initial pleasure has faded, we're left with death and shame.

James pulled no punches when he wrote, "Sin, when it is full-grown, gives birth to death" (James 1:15 NIV). When we act out, the outcome is always pain and shame.

- Instead of life, lust gives death.
- Instead of joy, lust gives shame.
- Instead of pleasure, lust gives pain.
- Instead of intimacy, lust gives isolation.

Sinful sexual behavior always leads to despair. Ask King David. After his illicit affair with Bathsheba, he murdered her husband, Uriah. Later the child that resulted from the affair died.

Ask Samson. After his affair with Delilah, he lost his sight and sacrificed his place of leadership in Israel.

Ask the men whose names appear in the newspapers every week, men who have sacrificed their families and reputations because they didn't say no to their lust.

But go further. Have you ever acted out in a sexually sinful way and escaped the consequences? Perhaps for a while.

But eventually you experienced loss. Nobody escapes the consequences of sexual sins. When we act out, we pay a high price.

But we don't have to sin. We can contain our lust and move forward with our life by breaking the cycle at its earliest stages.

Equipped to Help Others

It would be easy for you to wonder what good could come from your struggles with sexual lust. I understand how you feel. I look back on segments of my life with genuine regret. At times I wish I could erase them from my memory like segments of a videotape.

But I realize that my experiences — the struggles and failures — have deepened my dependence on God. They have helped me understand the suffering and struggles other men experience. Paul wrote, "Praise be to the God and Father of our Lord Jesus Christ, the Father of compassion and the God of all comfort, who comforts us in all our troubles, so that we can comfort those in any trouble with the comfort we ourselves have received from God" (2 Corinthians 1:3–4 NIV).

I thank God that through his Son he accepts us as we are. He sees our failures and loves us anyway. But he does more. He wraps us in the blanket of his comfort and heals our hurts. Then he enables us to offer that same blanket of comfort and healing to others.

That truth brings us to an important place. As you find comfort in God and seek to break the temptation cycle, there is another step you must take. In fact, I'm convinced that without it, you won't be able to stand for long. You need to connect with other men. You need to offer them the comfort and encouragement of the Lord, and you need to let them support you as you seek to live a pure life. In the next chapter you'll discover how to do that.

FOR DISCUSSION

1. What is a ritual?

2. What specific rituals do you have?

3. Why is it dangerous to allow even one seemingly innocent ritual exist in your life?

4. What specifically will you do to get rid of your rituals?

5. What is always the result of sexual sin?

6. How can God use your weakness to help others?

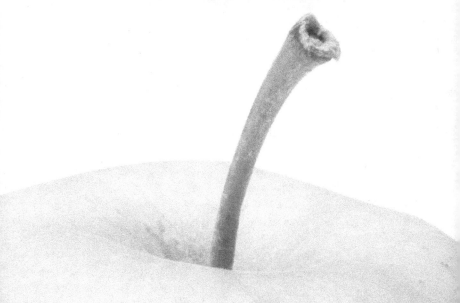

PART FOUR

LIVING FREE FOR THE REST OF YOUR LIFE

The Four Phases of Friendship

If you've ever watched *Home Improvement*, you know Tim Allen is a funny man. What you may not know is that he spent time in prison for selling drugs. How does he view his time behind bars? After reflecting on that question, he said, "Prison was the worst and the best thing that ever happened to me."[1]

In his bestselling book *Don't Stand Too Close to a Naked Man*, Allen tells about an experience he had while in jail. The event occurred right after he was placed in a holding cell with ten other guys. The first thing he noticed about the cell was that the toilet was in the middle of the room. He probably noticed that first because he had some business he needed to take care of. He said he looked at the can, then at the ceiling, then at the can, then at the ten guys in the cell. He wanted to leave. But the door was closed and locked.

He made up his mind that he would not use that can. No way! How could he take a dump with ten other guys watching? Finally, he wrote, "Digestion being as it is, things must emerge. I ambled tentatively to the can. I turned away and started back to my seat, but knew it was no good. I was committed. I sat down and suddenly all the men began moving toward me. I panicked.

"I didn't have to. This still blows my mind.

"What they did was form a horseshoe around me with their backs in my direction." Why had they done that? Allen said, "Because they're men, too. It was a big revelation. These aren't just losers like me, but they're men. They do this so you can have some privacy and no one can see in from the outside."[2]

That last statement is profound, because it describes what every man needs. We need friends who understand our fears and offer us protection, men who will stand guard around us during our times of vulnerability and shame.

It's too bad Allen had to go to jail to discover the willingness of men to shelter each other, to stand guard for each other. Because most men aren't forced into such close relationships, they never find out. As I've talked with men, I've discovered most of them feel that their struggles with sexual lust are personal. They're private. They're shameful. Like a trip to the can — it's not the sort of thing they want other men to see.

We're comfortable talking with men about inconsequential things like our golf game, the condition of our car, or our most recent vacation. But we resist talking about personal struggles and failures. Yet we need friends we can share our darkest sins and greatest triumphs with, friends who can help us stand when we're tempted and lift us up when we fall, friends we can support when they're in need.

David and Jonathan had that kind of friendship. After the death of Jonathan, David lamented, "I grieve for you, Jonathan my brother; you were very dear to me. Your love for me was wonderful, more wonderful than that of women" (2 Samuel 1:26 NIV).

That astounding statement expresses a truth known by just about every man. Namely, there are aspects of male friendship that are unlike — and better — than what men experience with women. Men know such friendships are possible, but they don't know how to experience them.

In this chapter, I want to examine the process from shallow friendships to best friends. And I want you to discover how you can cultivate deep friendships with other men. Friendships that will help you root your identity in Christ and encourage you to live a sexually pure life.

A Process You've Probably Never Thought About

Have you ever wondered how a friendship progresses from an acquaintance at work or church to the place where you would give your life for a guy? I never had. In fact, I never would have given it a second thought, or even a first one, if not for a book I read by Dr. Herb Goldberg entitled *The Hazards of Being Male*.

In his book Goldberg identifies what he calls the four phases of buddyship*. Actually, the word "buddy" isn't one that men use much nowadays. Goldberg likes the term because it speaks of youth and spontaneity. He believes that this, when combined with adult maturity, contains the potential for the "ultimate in masculine friendship."[3] In his eyes, a buddy is the ultimate friend ... a man you feel comfortable and at ease with, a man you love like a brother, a friend you'd sacrifice anything for.

The question Goldberg answers is, "How do we develop buddies?" His insight helps us know why we have so few and what we must do, or be willing to endure, to have one.

---

* I've kept with Dr. Goldberg's concept but changed the names of the friendship phases.

Back-Scratching Friends

Initially men connect with other men who can help them. It looks like this:

"Hey, Joe, will you loan me your new power drill?"

"Sure, and when you come over to pick it up would you mind dropping off that new electric buffer you bought the other day? I'm waxing my car this afternoon."

At work the back scratching involves taking care of another salesman's client, covering for a friend's mistake, and basically helping each other succeed. Because the benefits are high and the emotional cost low, most male friendships remain in this phase — and as long as both men benefit, the friendship prospers. When the mutual benefit ends, the friendship fades.

At times a back-scratching friendship at work can end badly. That occurs when one man is used by another and receives nothing in return or when he's tossed aside like an empty can once his usefulness is exhausted. One of the painful lessons some men have experienced at work is that when they lose their job, they also lose most of their work friends. "I thought we were good friends," they'll say. "We joked around every day. Sometimes we even hung out after work."

And they were friends ... back-scratching friends. What few men understand is that the mutual benefit of the friendship served as the glue that held it together. Take away the glue and the friendship falls apart.

Over a decade ago I left a church I had pastored for nine years. Even though I've stayed in the community, I seldom see most of my friends from the church. For all the attention they've given me after my departure, I could have died and been buried. No, that's not right. If I had died they would have attended my funeral. Back-scratching friends may not call you on the phone, but they will attend your funeral.

I'm not judging those people. After all, we're all that way. I suspect some of them wondered why I never gave them a call. It's not that I disliked them or tried to avoid them. When we would see each other at Home Depot or somewhere else, we'd always be cordial. But since we no longer have a reason to connect, we don't.

Until I read Goldberg's book, I always thought the sudden disappearance of my church friends seemed odd, and then I realized it was our common vision and service at the church that bound us together.

If you think about it, most of your friends are probably people who scratch your back while you scratch theirs. But Goldberg points out that from these friendships of mutual benefit another kind of friend may emerge.

Recreational Friends

These friends are guys we enter the male zone with. Our mutual interest in golf, racquetball, hunting, fishing, fixing up old cars, or coaching our kids throws us together on a regular basis. The activity provides the safe setting where we connect. Since the friendship revolves around the activity, there isn't a need for closeness. One strange thing about recreational friends is what may happen if you're sick and miss a foursome.

"I'm back," you say to the rest of your foursome. "Sorry, I missed last week."

"You missed last week?" one of them says.

"Yeah, I got sick. But I got Jake to fill in for me."

"Oh, yeah. I didn't even notice you weren't here. You okay now?"

"Yeah, I'm fine," you say as you tee up your ball.

Recreational friends seldom miss each other as long as someone else fills their spot, and they rarely discuss anything of greater importance than the latest football game. As strange as it sounds, men can play golf together for years and never know each other.

Close Friends

But something more can grow from recreational friends when two men have a natural affinity — that is, if they enjoy each other's company. In that case, they may become close friends. When that happens they can disagree without feeling they have to be right. They can play and neither has to win — although both want to. Close friends are men who genuinely celebrate each other's successes. Unlike a scratch-my-back or recreational amigo, this kind of a friend offers help when it's needed. They'll loan each other money or a car or even drive us to the airport.

If you remain close friends long enough, you'll have a chance for a friend to become more than a friend.

Buddies

The deepest friendship between men is seldom reached, because it follows a crisis. Many of us remember as kids becoming better friends with a guy after a fight. Similarly, we become buddies with a man only after our friendship has survived a crisis that threatens to destroy it.

Buddies are friends
who have survived
a relational crisis.

Back-Scratching Friends

▼

Recreational Friends

▼

Close Friends

▼

A Crisis Hits the Friendship

▼

Buddies

The breach is frequently created by an act of insensitivity or disrespect that, like a knife wound, inflicts deep pain. This act takes the mask off both men and reveals the sharp edges and abrasive lines that hadn't been seen before. The once-close friend's glaring weakness stands out like a wart on the tip of his nose. Both men are wounded and face the temptation to abandon each other. In fact, that's the easiest thing to do.

At this point the friendship is teetering on the brink of extinction. The two men will part and never be as close again — or they'll work through the crisis and become buddies. Growth occurs when they conclude the friendship is more important than their wounds. It takes place when each sees the weaknesses in his friend and decides to remain friends anyway.

Men who survive this crisis enter into a friendship that possesses deep trust. They know their buddy has seen them at their worst and accepts them anyway. It becomes a friendship in which at different times each serves as teacher, student, comforter, corrector, coach, and cheerleader. They now know they have a friend who will be there for them regardless of what happens.

Here's how Goldberg describes the friendship:

There is a sense of warmth and empathic understanding and comfort when one person is feeling weak, acting foolish, or being vulnerable. In these instances one buddy gets stability and nourishment from the other. There is a happy, mutual sharing of resources, both material and emotional. The competitive element is inconsequential and a win for one becomes a win for both. The brother-brother dimension of buddyship is one in which each looks out for the other, protecting him from exploitation.[4]

Several years ago my close friend, Bob Bobosky, and I faced a crisis that threatened our friendship. After the death of his mother he was overwhelmed with grief. Not being the sensitive type, I had no idea the loss had hurt him so deeply. When Bob turned to me for support, I listened and prayed and then quickly changed the subject. He was astounded by my insensitivity and got off the phone as fast as he could.

When I contacted him the next day he told me he needed some space. He said he needed time to process his loss. Later attempts to contact him were rebuffed. Looking back I knew that nothing in the history of our friendship had prepared me for this. In the past he had weathered losses with little emotion, and I had never suffered a personal loss that I could refer to as an emotional point of reference.

While our friendship had survived some past speed bumps, I became increasingly convinced this was a steel wall, not a speed bump. During the next year I determined that no matter how often he stiff-armed me, I wouldn't walk away.

A year after his mom's death, we sat in his office. "Thanks for never giving up on me," Bob said. "I've been harsh with you, yet you hung in there with me."

For the first time in a year, he reached out to me. I thank God neither of us gave up, because we're closer friends than before. In the past he had seen my insensitivity but never suffered from it. I had seen his ability to distance himself from people but never felt it myself. Because of this crisis we saw each other's rough edges. Yet we hung in there. We weathered the crisis of our friendship and emerged as buddies.

Once close friends become buddies they have a friendship without roles. Each man feels safe to act silly and stupid as well as serious and mature. He can be himself without fear of rejection. He can openly share his failures and victories, because he knows he's unconditionally accepted.

That experience changed my life. I now know that if someone has suffered a loss all of my energies must be focused on listening and caring instead of promoting my agenda. And since then, Bob, who used to pull away when annoyed, doesn't do that anymore. When I asked him why, he said, "I quit withdrawing because you said it hurt you."

> *Buddies absorb their friend's weaknesses*
> *and change because they see their own.*

Building Buddies

Most guys remember what it was like to have a buddy when they were a kid. But as adults, men talk about their need for an accountability group to help them keep the promises they've made to God and to their wife. They perceive an accountability group as a place where they report how things are going with their life. They don't think of it as a few buddies meeting because they love each other.

Since most groups begin at the "scratch my back" phase, this perception shouldn't surprise us. Men get together in accountability groups because it's mutually beneficial for everyone present. They aren't meeting because they like each other. They may not even know one another.

Initially a man will attend with the best of intentions. He wants to be sexually pure. He wants to be open about his life. He wants to show up at all the meetings.

But it's hard to meet with a group of guys he doesn't know very well. It's hard to be open with men he doesn't yet trust. It's hard to lean on other men when he wants to appear strong.

If he falls into sin, he'll want to skip the meeting. That way he can retain his image of spirituality. Sadly, he may never return. Sadder still, nobody may search him out.

But someone must search him out. He needs a friend who will hunt him down. And so do you. You need several close friends you feel safe around. Friends who will be there for you no matter what you say or do. Friends who will help you work through your struggles. Friends who will coach and comfort you. And friends you'll do the same thing for.

It's those kinds of friendships that make accountability work because the men care about each other. They'll check up on you because they love you — they want you to succeed. And you feel the same way about them.

Such friendships don't develop after a meeting or two. Remember, it takes time to move from scratch-my-back friends to buddies. And the road may be bumpy. But as I've reflected on the kind of men I'd want as friends, and the kind of man I want to be, I've identified four crucial traits that we'll examine in the next chapter.

FOR DISCUSSION

1. What are the four phases of male friendship? What characterizes each one?

2. What is the transition that moves men from friends to buddies? Can you think of times when you had a friendship that didn't make it through the transition? Do you have friendship that did survive the transition? What was the outcome?

3. Why do men need male buddies?

4. How long does it take to become buddies? Why?

5. What can you do to cultivate closer friends? How do you plan on doing that?

What to Look for in a Friend

At a men's event in New York I sat on the front row and listened as author, educator, and clinical psychologist Dr. Rod Cooper spoke on the importance of having close friends. To illustrate his point he told a story about an African-American boy he knew.

He said the kid felt excited when he joined the Boy Scouts. His enthusiasm seemed especially justified when one day at the end of a long march his troop leader said, "I'm going to reward you boys with a trip to the swimming pool."

A short time later his Boy Scout troop lined up at the gate of a pool to pay their entrance fee. When it was the black boy's turn to pay, the attendant stopped him, "Son, are you black or do you just have a good tan?"

Embarrassed, the boy said nothing.

"Since I'm not sure," the attendant said, "you can't swim here. This is a private pool for white people."

The Scout leader urged the boy to walk home, but the rest of the kids declared that if he didn't swim, they wouldn't swim. So they all went to a public beach.

That incident left a deep impression on the boy. He grew up believing black skin was a handicap. To succeed he thought he'd have to outperform everyone else — just to compensate for his skin color.

So that kid became good, real good. He played the trumpet and became the number one high school trumpeter in Ohio. He graduated in the top five of his class. He went to college and, once again, was at the top of his field. Still there was an uneasiness about him because he was constantly trying to deny part of himself. He performed well, but he couldn't get close to anyone because they might reject him for being black. He also got angry because he felt alone. He was a black man trying to make it in a white world.

He thought going to seminary would help because he'd be around other believers, but the sting of prejudice found him there too, since he was one of only three blacks on campus. In spite of the fact that he felt alone and angry his drive for perfection won him the distinction as the best preacher in his class — he won the preaching award.

After seminary he moved to Houston, Texas, where he began his first ministry. One day, almost by "accident," he met a white guy, a pastor. This man talked openly about his struggles and victories. After they had become close friends the pastor took a big risk. In fact he put the entire friendship on the table and threw the dice. He told his black friend that he could see through his performance mentality that drove him to cover up his blackness. He said he admired the fact that he was black.

Then Rod told his audience the identity of the African-American man. He was speaking about himself. And his friend was me.

He went on to say, "One day Bill invited me over for dinner. He sat me down, put his hands on my shoulders, looked me straight in the eyes, and said, 'Rod, I thank God for your blackness. It's not a handicap. God didn't make a mistake.

Thank him right now for all of who you are — your blackness included.'"

As Rod continued with his message, he said, "I struggled and squirmed, and then I broke into tears. And then I bowed my head and said, 'Thank you, Jesus for making me who I am — for making all of me.' I stood up, and Bill and I hugged, and I continued to cry. Finally, I had accepted myself for who I was — all of me. Then Bill said, 'I love you, Rod.'"

At that point in the sermon, Rod stopped, pointed a finger at me and said, "I love that man. I love you, Bill Perkins."

When Rod spoke those words I started crying — right there on the front row at a men's event in upstate New York.[1]

Rod and I have been friends a long time, and he knows how indebted I am to him — I'm convinced my present ministry exists because he opened the door for me.

Over the years we've had some struggles, but by the grace of God, we've hung in there. As I've thought about the traits Rod and I saw in each other, and what we ask of other men, I've narrowed it down to the four most important. I believe these are the traits you should look for in a man you hope will become a buddy some day. These are the traits you should cultivate in yourself so you'll be a good friend to other men.

FRIENDSHIP TRAIT ONE: A Bold Faith in God

There's no greater friendship found in the pages of the Bible than Jonathan and David's. The first recorded instance of the two men meeting occurred after David killed Goliath. I'm convinced it was David's bold faith that attracted Jonathan.

While Jonathan was King Saul's son, what set him apart wasn't his royal lineage, but his courageous faith. Before David's historic one-on-one battle with Goliath, Jonathan and his armor bearer had taken on and defeated twenty Philistines. Prior to the fight, Jonathan told his helper, "Nothing can hinder the LORD from saving, whether by many or by few" (1 Samuel 14:6 NIV).

The words of Jonathan were similar to those David yelled at Goliath when he said, "You come against me with sword and spear and javelin, but I come against you in the name of the LORD Almighty, the God of the armies of Israel, whom you have defied. This day the LORD will hand you over to me" (1 Samuel 17:45–46 NIV).

When Jonathan heard David and saw his heroic faith, he knew that was the man he wanted for a friend. And he determined to do all he could to cultivate the friendship.

Because your battle for purity
is essentially a spiritual one,
you need buddies whose faith
will raise the bar for you.

You need men who will challenge and comfort you. That's why you should look for buddies who are devoted to Christ. They don't have to be perfect, and they won't be, but they need to have a passion to grow stronger.

It's their commitment that will prompt you to take the necessary steps to assure your purity. I mentioned earlier that after watching my nude neighbor talk on the phone, I confessed what I had done to my Saturday morning band of brothers. When two of them said they had been peering at a neighbor for an extended time, I knew I had to take a bold step or the same thing would happen to me.

After the meeting I drove to my neighbor's house and rang the doorbell. Because we lived behind each another, I had never met them. Wanting to be truthful without incriminating myself, or getting shot, I came up with something I could say that would protect my reputation and also remove the temptation.

A moment after I rang the doorbell, my neighbor opened the door. "Yeah," he said.

"Hello. I'm Bill Perkins and I live behind you." I relaxed a little when I saw he wasn't carrying a chainsaw and wearing a hockey mask. "I wanted to alert you to a possible danger we may have in our neighborhood."

That got his attention.

"A couple of weeks ago a neighbor woman told my wife she had seen a man peeking through her window one night" (yes, this actually happened).

"No kidding?"

"No kidding."

"That's weird."

"I thought so. Anyway, I got concerned when I noticed my dog barking when I let her out at night. I haven't seen anyone in my yard, but I wouldn't want it used as a platform to invade your privacy. I was thinking you might want to keep your shades down at night."

"Thanks for telling me," he said. "I've got two teenage daughters and just a week ago one of them went onto our deck to sunbathe. The moment she stepped outside she saw a man looking through one of our windows. He jumped over the fence and ran away. You can bet we'll keep our shades down at night."

That was a tough visit to make, and yet it harnessed my lust. But it did more than that. It provided me with an opportunity to challenge my friends to take similar action — which they later did. I thanked God that after leaving the meeting with my friends, while I felt strong, I took aggressive action to protect myself from a time of future weakness.

Without my band of brothers, friends I could fess up to, I don't know what might have happened. Ultimately, it was our passion for Christ that prompted each of us to take that difficult step, and it was our friendship that infused us with courage.

FRIENDSHIP TRAIT TWO: Loyalty

At some point in a friendship, you'll have to make a commitment to stick with your friend no matter what the cost. Jonathan did that with David. He made a covenant with him that was based on a mutual understanding and agreement (1 Samuel 18:1–4). They vowed to be true and loyal friends for the rest of their lives.

As a symbol of his commitment, Jonathan gave David a valuable gift. Because he was a prince, Jonathan was one of the few men in Israel with a sword. He gave David not only this but also his bow, belt, robe, and tunic. Jonathan gave David his most valuable possessions. In doing so, he was saying, "All I have is yours."

Talk about devotion! While you and I don't have a sword, bow, and belt, we do have something of great value we can give a buddy: time. There's nothing you can give away that's worth more than your time. I've found that I don't have to give it away in large chunks, but I need to make weekly phone calls, send emails to see how they're doing, and be available if they want someone to talk with. I must to be willing to drop anything I'm doing for them.

One day I faced something I didn't think would ever happen to me. In spite of the fact that I led a rapidly growing church, my board indicated they thought it was time for me to move on. Some of them believed my writing ministry was distracting me from the church.

Emotionally devastated, I called one of my buddies. After cracking a few jokes, just to lighten the load, he said, "I'll pick you up in the morning, and we'll spend the day together."

"But I thought you had to fly to San Diego to close that shopping-center deal," I replied.

"I did — but not anymore," he said. "Something more important just came up."

That's the kind of loyalty buddies show each other.

Jonathan did that for David in two ways.

First, he ran interference for him. When Jonathan's father, King Saul, was trying to kill David, the young prince spoke with his father about David's innocence. Later he helped David escape the king's wrath (1 Samuel 19:1–7; 20:1–42).

Buddies take time to defend each other.

Second, he encouraged David in the Lord. Exhausted by King Saul's relentless pursuit, the giant-killer despaired. Seeking refuge, David and his band of men hid in a cave in the desert hills of Ziph.

Jonathan knew his friend was depressed, and he knew where to find him. Disregarding the wrath of his father, Jonathan snuck into David's presence and offered him hope. The prince told his friend, "Don't be afraid.... My father Saul will not lay a hand on you. You will be king over Israel, and I will be second to you. Even my father Saul knows this" (1 Samuel 23:17 NIV).

That brief encounter was the last time David would see his friend alive. But what an encounter! Jonathan reminded David that God would one day make him king. In saying that, Jonathan assured his friend that in spite of his current situation, God's purpose for his life would be fulfilled.

Buddies take time to encourage their friends in the Lord.

Maintaining moral purity is a daily battle. It's one that requires loyalty. When I sense that one of my buddies is hiding in a cave, I go after him. When they sense I'm withdrawing, they come after me. Why? Because withdrawal is the first sign that a man is beginning to yield. At such times we need to follow Jonathan's example. We need to go after our buddies and strengthen them in the Lord — and we need to allow them to do that for us.

The question is, how can we do that in the area of sexual purity?

FRIENDSHIP TRAIT THREE: **A Shared Purpose**

A number of years ago while enjoying lunch with a friend I asked, "How are you doing with porn when you're on the road?"

Taken back by my directness, he smiled. "Why do you ask?"

"Because when I'm on the road, I'm tempted and wondered if you were too."

"I'm not doing well," he said, "but I want to."

The next week he joined two other guys and me for a weekly Tuesday morning meeting. Over the years we came up with a list of six commitments that are crucial to a healthy group. They describe the characteristics of a man I want to hang with. I think they would be the kind of guys you want as friends and buddies too. As I've reflected on the six commitments, I think they reveal a deeply held driving purpose: *allowing Christ to live his life through us.*

A man makes them because he wants his new identity in Christ to be fleshed out in his life. Here they are:

1. Committed to Christ, his family, and a life of sexual purity.

2. Committed to the men in the group and to the reality that every man is just as messed up and vulnerable as the other men in the group. This commitment creates safety for every man and infuses him with dignity.

3. Committed to confidentiality. Every man promises never to discuss with anyone outside the group what's talked about inside the group — unless a child has been violated or a crime is being planned.

4. Committed to tell the truth when asked specific questions. No man will lie to another member of the group.

5. Committed to the reality that every man in the group, including himself, wants to hide his sin. Because of that, each man gives permission to the other men to ask specific questions about sinful behavior, questions that cannot be evaded. And they expect the same from the rest of the group.

6. Committed to identify the rituals that precede acting out and share them with the group so they can check up on how he's doing.

With these commitments in mind, begin looking for a friend or two you can meet with. Identify someone you think shares your devotion to Christ. Pick someone you sense wants to be pure. Ask if he's interested in meeting on a regular basis for mutual support and encouragement.

During the first meeting let him know you're interested in cultivating a friendship that will help you keep your promises to God, to your wife, and to your children. Let him know you need the support of a friend to be pure and you thought he might feel the same way.

Be careful to move one step at a time. You don't need to dump your entire load during the first meeting. As you open up and share your struggles, give him time to feel safe so he can share his. As you talk about the temptations you face, remember that your goal isn't to support each other in failure. Your goal is to challenge each other to godliness.

When you discuss the commitments I mentioned above, be sure to make it clear that neither of you is using them to control the other. Discuss them. Reword them. Make them your own. The sooner you do this, the better. Once you both accept them, you'll have permission to share more openly and probe more aggressively.

It may not take long for something to go wrong. He may begin to make excuses for missing the meetings or not returning phone calls. When that occurs, you'll probably ask, "What happened? Things were going so well."

FRIENDSHIP TRAIT FOUR: A Willingness to Get Past "What Happened?"

It's easy at times like that to just move on without him. But remember, a crisis in the friendship may be God's way of turning a friend into a buddy. That's why it's crucial for you to follow the example of Jesus with Peter.

Following his denial of the Lord, Peter was overwhelmed with grief. After hearing about the resurrection and seeing the empty tomb, what do you think was running through his mind? He must have wondered if the Lord would ever want to see him again.

Jesus wasted no time. After the resurrection, he appeared alone to Peter, and while we don't know what the two discussed, it's not hard to guess (Luke 24:34). At a later meeting on the seashore, Jesus assured Peter of his strategic role in the kingdom of God (John 21:15–18).

Peter accepted the Lord's forgiveness and learned from his mistake. I suspect that's why he expressed genuine compassion toward others. He urged us to "be sympathetic, love as brothers, be compassionate and humble" (1 Peter 3:8 NIV). Peter had learned firsthand about the value of those traits, and he learned it from a sin he committed that created a crisis in his relationship with Jesus. A crisis Jesus refused to ignore. A crisis the Lord addressed by meeting with Peter.

If a friend stumbles he may be embarrassed to see you. It's your responsibility to pursue him. Remember, you both made a commitment to the reality that every man wants to hide, and because of that commitment he's agreed to speak the truth when asked specific questions. You've got to meet with him to ask those questions. By going after him you're proving the seriousness of your commitment to him.

Once the two of you finally connect, assure him of your acceptance. Remind him that each man in the group agreed that all of you have issues. Nobody's perfect. Everyone's in process.

After you sense he feels safe, ask him: "Have you done anything you shouldn't have since we last met?"

If he admits to a misdeed, affirm his honesty, and then try to trace the source of his fall. Ask him which ritual got him back on the "slippery slope." Try to devise a strategy to avoid letting it happen again. Give him hope that if he can increase the gap between falls eventually he'll stop falling altogether. But he can't give up just because he blew it.

Remember, a key to purity is cutting off lust at the preoccupation and ritualization stages. It's your job to help your buddy do that, and when he stumbles, it's your job to help him get back up. His job is to be there for you.

Don't Give Up

I once asked my band of brothers, "How do you think you'd be doing if we weren't here for you?"

"I can't imagine," one of them said.

"I know I'd have fallen into serious sin by now," another commented.

It's impossible for me to put into words how much I love those guys. I can't express how their comfort and confrontation have been used by God in my life. I want that for you. And I want you to know that it won't come easily because men resist close friendships. You'll have to persevere while the friendship grows, and in the process you'll probably be growled at and bitten.

I'm reminded of the story of the man who saw a two-month-old black Labrador retriever lying in a puddle of mud under a bridge. It had a gash on its head, and its front legs were raw and swollen where they had been bound with a rope.

The man cautiously approached the puppy. When he was a few steps away, the dog bared its teeth and snarled. The man reached into his pocket and pulled out a strip of beef jerky. He squatted in front of the dog, talked to it softly, and tossed it a sliver of meat.

After several minutes he was petting the dog on the head and untying the tattered rope from its injured front legs. He then carried the dirty dog home, nursed its wounds, and gave it food, water, and a soft bed.

The next morning when the man approached the dog, it snarled and snapped at him. Determined to befriend the animal, the man talked softly and gave it a piece of ham. Day after day he worked patiently with the Lab. Finally, weeks later, as the man was watching TV the dog padded over to his chair and licked the back of his hand. The man looked down and saw the Lab smiling and wagging his tail.

I believe a lot of guys are like that dog. They've been wounded and bound by the world. They're suspicious of others and try to keep them at a safe distance. We're responsible to demonstrate consistent love and kindness. If we want a buddy, we have to commit ourselves to a lifetime of loyalty and trust. We have to be willing to endure his growls and bites. But if we hang in there, one day we'll realize we have a buddy, someone who feels safe with us and with whom we feel safe, someone who helps us be morally pure while we help them do the same thing.

> *I've got to say that I'm living proof*
> *that what my friends do as buddies,*
> *they do well.*
> *And I hope they feel that way about me too.*

Of course, there is another relationship that is crucial if we're going to be pure, and that's the one we share with our wife. We'll discuss that relationship in the next chapter.

FOR DISCUSSION

1. Why is commitment to God an important trait of a friend?

2. How did Jonathan show his commitment to David?

3. What one thing can you give a friend to show your commitment? How have you done that in the past? How will you do that in the future?

4. What two things did Jonathan do to show his support for David? How could you do that for a friend?

5. Review the commitments made by a group of men dedicated to helping each other maintain purity. Which is the most important to you? Why?

For Married Men Only

It's hot outside because it's September in Austin. Not as hot as Phoenix in the summer but more humid and sticky. Cindy and I are cleaning our matchbox-size apartment that's on Cedar Street by the campus of the University of Texas. The phone rings. It's one of those black plastic jobs with a dialer that looks like a clock with holes over the numbers. I pick up the receiver.

"Hello," I say.

"Hi! I'm Diane Dawson." The caller talks with a sweet southern drawl. "We met at a party at Joe Glickman's house in Dallas. I told you I'd call when I came to Austin. Well, I'm here and hoped we could get together."

I remember Diane. She's tall and slender with dark hair and a nice figure. "I'm flattered you called, but I got married last month."

"Oh," she says, disappointed. "I guess that means you're not available any longer. Right?"

I sense from the way she said "right?" that maybe she thinks after four weeks of marriage I'm ready for a break. "Yeah, that's right," I say. "But thanks for calling."

I hang up the phone and am hit with the profound reality that for the rest of my life I would never date, kiss, hug, or have sex with a woman besides my wife. I swallow hard.

"Who was that?" Cindy asks.

"Diane Dawson."

"Who's that?"

"A girl I met at Joe's."

"What did she want?"

"A date."

"A date?"

"Right. I told her I was married and madly in love with my wife who happens to be the most beautiful and sexy woman alive."

"I didn't hear you say that."

"Well, maybe I didn't. But that's why I married you."

Cindy smiles, wraps her arms around me, and squeezes.

Yes, I felt I had married the most beautiful and sexy woman alive. But keeping the fizz in our sex life has been a life-long challenge. Like most guys, I've found that married sex can get boring. Many men miss the excitement of hunting for a woman and exploring new territory. They tire of doing the same thing with the same woman over and over and over again. When boredom infects a man's sex life at home, he may look for excitement elsewhere.

So far we've talked about how you can keep from committing sexual sins. That's half the battle. The other half involves finding sexual pleasure at home with your wife. In this chapter I'll share with you some ideas that will restore passion to your marriage. If you're single, I hope these insights will give you something to look forward to when you marry.

God's Guidelines for Dynamic Sex

Most men would never look to the Bible as a coaching manual for good sex. And at first glance Paul's instructions concerning sex may seem superficial. But upon closer examination they provide four practical guidelines that will vitalize your sex life at home.

GUIDELINE ONE: **Your Body Belongs to Your Wife**

Paul said, "The husband should fulfill his marital duty to his wife, and likewise the wife to her husband. The wife's body does not belong to her alone but also to her husband. In the same way, the husband's body does not belong to him alone but also to his wife" (1 Corinthians 7:3–4 NIV).

You may read that passage and say, "Yes! I own my wife's body. She must do whatever I ask whenever I ask and how ever often I ask. This is definitely a passage *she* must memorize. It's a passage I'll definitely help *her* put into practice."

Umm ... I hate to break the news to you, but you've completely missed the point. Paul was talking to your wife, not you. He said *she* should regard her body as belonging to you, her husband.

But he also had something to say to you. Namely, *you're* to regard your body as belonging to her.

You and your wife must remember that you're there for each other. She must see herself as your sexual servant. And you must see yourself as hers. Paul is describing a sexual attitude that's focused on the other person.

In light of that fact you should never tell your wife, "God says you're here for me."

Instead you should tell her, "God says I'm here for you."

This is a crucial concept. It implies your sexual energies are for no one else. They belong to your wife alone and should always be focused on her, not another woman or the image of another woman.

As we saw in chapter one, it's normal for you to be sexually attracted to other women. God wired you that way. But you must exercise discipline. The next time you see a woman and find your lust getting a foothold, tell yourself, "I'm glad God created beautiful women and gave me the ability to enjoy them. But I belong to my wife." Remember that the new man in you, the good man, delights in pleasing God and your wife.

Instead of fantasizing about another woman, use the moment of sexual interest to focus attention on your wife. Remind yourself that your body belongs to her, and that includes your mind and your eyes.

GUIDELINE TWO: **Meet Your Wife's Sexual Needs**

This guideline flows logically from the previous one. If I'm here for my wife, it makes sense that it's my responsibility to meet her sexual needs. What's fascinating to me is that nothing turns on a man more than an aroused wife. We derive pleasure by pleasuring our wives.

The problem is most men forget that their wives are women. I don't mean anatomically, of course. I mean in terms of what turns them on. We tend to do for our wives what we want done for us.

Of course, our wives do the same thing. If we're going to take Paul's admonition seriously, we need to discover what arouses our wives and do that for them. Since I can't possibly cover everything women like in one chapter, let's look at some of the most important things we can do to sexually stimulate our wives and in the process add some octane to the passion in our marriages.

Stay in First Gear!

I'll never forget teaching my youngest son, Paul, how to drive my shiny black, brand new and very fast Porsche. Actually, it was a five-speed Mazda — gutless — Miata that I wish was a Porsche. Anyway, watching him try to get the timing down between the clutch and accelerator was as fun as a carnival ride. I had forgotten how jer–jer–jerky a ride could be when the driver can't coordinate releasing the clutch with pushing down the gas pedal.

I also had forgotten the difficulty a new driver has knowing *when* to shift gears. Initially Paul would shift from first to second and then to third before he had enough RPMs to propel the car forward. As he drove up Overlook, a steep hill a few blocks from our home, the car rolled to a stop before reaching the summit. Once that happened he faced the additional challenge of coordinating the gas pedal and clutch while the car was rolling downhill … backward.

And I faced the challenge of not freaking out. Oh, the joys of fatherhood!

Of course, it didn't take long for him to get the timing down. Unfortunately, a lot of men never achieve that same level of success with their wives. Many men want to move from first to fifth gear with a woman before she has enough sexual energy built up to reach the summit. The reason we do that is because our sexual tachometer is redlining after five minutes, and we want to shift gears.

One afternoon Cindy and I were involved in foreplay, and she was slowly caressing my shoulders, back, neck, head, arms, and hands. When she had caressed all those body parts she caressed them again. As I endured her lovemaking, I thought, "If I'd wanted a rubdown, I'd have gone to a masseuse." Fortunately, I kept that thought to myself.

Why was she caressing me like that? Because it's what she wanted from me. Since her engine was hitting 1,000 RPMs, she needed me to move slowly with her and not shift gears until she was closer to the redline.

If you want to meet your wife's sexual needs, stay in first gear until you sense she's ready for you to shift gears. Move slowly. Give her time to warm up.

> *Remember:*
> *going slow = great sex.*

It will help if you know what she likes. Don't make the mistake of assuming she likes something just because you've done it ten thousand times. Find out what arouses her. Learn exactly where and how she likes to be touched, and find out how fast she wants you to move along.

You might try playing a game Cindy and I engage in from time to time. Your wife will love it. Select an evening when you won't be disturbed. Inform your wife in advance that you're going to make love to her according to *her* direction. Every touch and move will be at the pace and place of her selection. As your lovemaking progresses, remember: the goal isn't your gratification but hers. Find out how she likes her breasts, stomach, inner thighs, and clitoris caressed.

Follow Her Instructions

You'll probably discover that she likes you to remain in each gear far longer than you prefer. But do it. Slow down. Be especially open to instructions concerning how to stimulate her clitoris — this is her pleasure point and it must be stimulated for her to achieve an orgasm. A failure to do so would give her as much pleasure as you'd get out of sex if your penis wasn't stroked.

When God made the clitoris, he took all the sensitive nerve endings in the penis, compressed them into a tiny point, and wrapped them in soft tissue. The clitoris is far more sensitive than the penis and must be touched gently. Even so, in most cases once a woman's clitoris is being stimulated, through intercourse or with your hand or her hand or a toy, it still takes longer for her to achieve an orgasm than it would you.

You'll likely discover that your wife won't want direct stimulation of her clitoris until she's wet. It's uncomfortable for the clitoris to be caressed when it's dry. Moisture around a woman's vagina is a sign of sexual arousal. (If she's dry, use a lubricant like KY Jelly or massage oil.)

Amazingly, even Solomon made poetic reference to his bride's excitement and her secretion of fluid. He wrote, "You are a garden fountain, a well of flowing water streaming down from Lebanon" (Song of Songs 4:15 NIV). It's fascinating that under divine inspiration he praised the beauty and scent of his sexually aroused bride (Song of Songs 4:13–14).

As you become more proficient in sexually stimulating your wife, she'll become more aroused. As that happens, your own level of pleasure will increase. As I said earlier, nothing turns men on more than a sexually excited wife. So if you want to experience the fun of an aroused wife, discover what turns her on.

Emotional Orgasms?

It may surprise you to hear that a woman doesn't have to achieve an orgasm to feel satisfied. While in seminary, the wives of seminary students met periodically to hear inspirational speakers. On one occasion the microphone was made available for women to share brief testimonies.

After the meeting Cindy came home and could hardly wait to tell me what had happened. She said a young woman had stepped up to the microphone and announced she was about to say something that would take a lot of pressure off some of the wives. Speaking with the enthusiasm of a scientist who just found a cure for cancer, she said, "I always thought an orgasm was physical. Last night I had an emotional orgasm, and now I know they aren't physical but emotional."

Cindy and I both laughed, because we knew that someday that woman would probably have a big-time physical orgasm and be embarrassed about her announcement. But on second thought we realized she had made a good point. It's possible for women to derive real pleasure out of sex without having an orgasm every time.

As guys, we can't imagine that. Why? Because for us sex provides a release of sexual energy. If we engage in foreplay and don't have an orgasm it can hurt. On the other hand, if the sexual tension in a woman doesn't build up to the point where she feels a need for an orgasm, don't pressure her into having one.

Crock-Pot Sex

Once you've discovered the pace and places that turn on your wife, try not to drive the same route every time you get together. As guys, we tend to get a technique down and repeat it over and over again. That's okay, but be sure to have several techniques you can use.

One of them is "Crock-Pot sex." That's the kind of sex that takes all day and night to cook. It begins in the morning with an extra-long hug and kiss as you leave, along with a promise to take her out to dinner. It's followed up with a phone call that communicates affection. Next comes a card or flower(s).

Remember:
a hug in the morning = great sex in the evening.

Notice I used the word "flower(s)." I did that because several years ago I discovered that every romantic act earns me one point with my wife. Both a single rose and a dozen roses are worth one point. Once I learned this, I decided to add up the points with more frequent and less expensive gifts.

Anyway, bring home a flower or a bunch of flowers. Put them in a vase and give her a kiss. I've learned over the years that Cindy loves to go for a walk with me. If your wife likes to go for walks with you, go for a walk.

Remember:
long walks in the park = great sex in the bedroom.

If you have kids, be sure and line up a babysitter for the evening. Remember, for your wife's sexual juices to heat up, she needs to be free of pressure. During dinner tell her how much you love her, how much she means to you. If you're a less expressive man, tell her anyway.

Remember:
words of affection all day = great sex at night.

Even a casual reading of Song of Songs reveals Solomon's frequent expressions of affection and appreciation for his bride. If you don't know what to say, here are some suggestions.

"You're beautiful."

"I'm glad I get to share my life with you."

"You have gorgeous eyes."

"I love to kiss your lips."

"Your kiss tastes sweet to me."

"I love to look at and caress your legs."

"I can't wait to touch you all over."

"I can't wait to feel your body against mine."

(By the way — it would be best to memorize the above statements or make up your own. Reading the list from a book will not work with most women. Especially if she's standing in front of you.)

When you get home, take a bubble bath or shower together. After you've dried each other off, give her a massage and allow her to give you one. Once you get in bed, remember — go slow. Wait until her RPMs have approached the redline before shifting gears.

Of course, Crock-Pot sex isn't something you can do daily or weekly. But once a month would earn you some major points with your wife.

Remember:
going slow = great sex.

Okay, I realize that the sex formulas I stated above don't guarantee great sex. But what I'm trying to hammer into your head is that for your wife sex is more than an orgasm. It includes a morning hug, long walks, words of affirmation, and slow foreplay. We tend to view those activities as the price we pay for sex. That's because we see sex as an act. Our wives see it as a dance and all of those acts are crucial steps.

Gourmet Sex

While Crock-Pot sex is great, it takes place at home. Occasionally you need to plan a getaway with your wife to a romantic spot. It doesn't have to be expensive. But it needs to be a place that makes her feel special.

For one of Cindy's birthdays I surprised her with an overnight stay in an executive suite of a local hotel. Before we went out for dinner, I had her pack an overnight case. I bought a bunch of inexpensive flowers at a local grocery store (they still counted as one point) and had a friend take them to the hotel before we arrived. When Cindy entered the room, the flower arrangement greeted her from its perch on a coffee table.

From that moment on all I needed to do was go sloooooow. The rest of the night was devoted to caring for her.

Microwave Sex

If you're willing to give your wife Crock-Pot sex and gourmet sex on a regular basis, she'll probably be willing to provide you with "microwave sex." In fact, it might be a dish she'd occasionally like herself. On those occasions when time is short, let her know you don't have time to fix a Crock-Pot but would sure like it if she would be willing to let you throw something in the microwave oven.

Of course, microwave sex comes in a variety of packages. They include intercourse, manual stimulation of the husband by the wife, mutual manual stimulation, oral sex, or sex with a toy. You and your wife need to feel free to do whatever turns you on, as long as it doesn't stimulate sinful lust or violate your conscience.

If this is the only meal on the menu, your wife won't be too excited about it. But if she knows you're committed to giving her what she needs, she'll enjoy taking care of your needs in this way. And if you become skilled at caressing her clitoris, she may achieve an orgasm every time you do. In fact, she may achieve several.

GUIDELINE THREE: **Don't Deny Your Wife**

In his excellent book *Mars and Venus in the Bedroom*, John Gray observes, "Biologically and hormonally, men are much more driven to be sexual than women are. Quite naturally, it is on their minds more of the time. Because a man is wanting it so much, he will feel rejected more of the time when he is not getting it."[1]

The instinctive response when a man feels rejected is withdrawal. A man's spirit reminds me of the sea urchins that are found in tide pools on the Oregon coast. These beautiful creatures look like an open flower. But the moment a stick probes their soft center, the sea urchin will clamp shut.

Our wives can do a lot of things to communicate whether or not they are interested in sex — and we know how to read every signal. Do they face us or face away from us when they come to bed? Do they complain about exhaustion or say they feel affectionate? Are they wearing sexy bedclothes or their old cotton nightgown? Do they tell us they have to get up early in the morning, or do they feel rested? Do they lock the door and put on romantic music before coming to bed or set the alarm clock? Once we begin to caress them, do they say, "That tickles," "My skin is sensitive tonight," "That doesn't feel good," or "Ouch!"

Because a man is so sensitive about sex, any lack of interest by his wife is like a stick in the spirit — it can shut him down. When that happens, a man will be hesitant to make any more advances. Over time he may not want sex with his wife. As Jay said in my office, "It's less of a hassle to masturbate."

We need to understand that the actions of our wife aren't usually intended as a sign of personal rejection. They may not even mean she's not interested in making love.

Sometimes when I ask Cindy if she's "in the mood," she'll say, "I don't know." When we first got married, I thought that meant, "No!" Later I discovered she meant she didn't know. Once I realized that, I followed her lack of interest with a gentle hug.

Guess what? More often than not she was in neutral and just needed me to patiently get her into first gear.

It may be that your sex drive is greater than your wife's. You may want sex three times a day, while twice a day is enough for her (don't you wish). But seriously, the differences in your appetite may cause you to frequently feel rejected. It's important to understand that your wife is probably not rejecting you. Her need simply isn't as great as yours. It's important to realize that God may have brought you together because he knew your wife needed the extra affection you could give her due to your additional sexual energy.

Regardless of why we feel rejected and hurt, we're not to sexually withdraw from our wives. To do so is sin. We're to take the time to meet their sexual needs, even when we feel like pulling away.

GUIDELINE FOUR: **Cultivate a Spiritual Connection**

Paul said, "Do not deprive each other except by mutual consent and for a time, so that you may devote yourselves to prayer. Then come together again so that Satan will not tempt you because of your lack of self-control" (1 Corinthians 7:5 NIV).

I've read scores of books about sex, and I've never once read anything about this particular verse. Yet I think it's critical for the sexual health of a husband and wife. Why? Because your physical relationship is intended by God to be a picture of your spiritual union. Nothing brings a couple closer to each other than prayer. Because God knows this, he says the only time you should abstain from sex is when you both agree to devote yourselves to prayer individually and as a couple.

The sad truth is that most men seldom pray with their wives. I'm not sure why. It may be because they feel spiritually inferior to their wives. Perhaps they don't think their prayers sound all that spiritual. Maybe they're just busy and don't think they have the time.

Whether or not you're in the habit of praying with your wife, I want to challenge you to try an experiment for one month. Every night before you go to sleep, pray with her. It doesn't have to be a long prayer, but make it real. In other words, don't recite a prayer you memorized as a child. Talk to God with your wife. Talk about the needs in your life, in your marriage, and in your family.

I suspect you'll be surprised at the immediate benefits your marriage will reap. For one thing, the two of you will feel much closer.

Next, set aside a time to abstain from sex so you can pray together. The period of abstinence needs to be related to how frequently you have sex. If you have sex every day, breaking for five days will be a significant time. If you have sex once a week, two weeks will be a challenge. Don't stop so long that you're tempted to satisfy yourself or look somewhere else for gratification.

This time of prayer will focus your life on the Lord, draw you together, and intensify your sexual appetite. It will cleanse you of any bitterness and renew your love. When you come back together again, you'll feel like newlyweds.

Enjoy God's Gift

For our twenty-fifth anniversary Cindy and I spent ten days in Hawaii. While we were there, we noticed scores of newlyweds. They were easy to spot, because of the way they held hands, walked arm in arm, and gazed into each other's eyes.

As I watched a couple in the hotel lobby, I said, "Let's pretend we're newlyweds."

"How do we do that?" Cindy asked.

"It's easy, all we have to do is hang all over each other like we did when we dated."

So Cindy and I glued ourselves together during our "honeymoon" in Hawaii. And why not? After twenty-five years we were certainly more in love than any other couple in Hawaii.

Now here's the kicker ... the more we expressed physical affection, the more affectionate we felt. The more we expressed our love verbally, the more love we felt.

I'm convinced there is nothing you can do to maintain sexual purity that's more important than loving your wife. Treat her as you did during your courtship, and you'll discover that some of the old fires are still there — they just need to be stroked ... I mean stoked.

Remember, when the home fire burns hot, the campfire isn't as appealing. Your job is to keep those home fires burning.

FOR DISCUSSION

1. What are the four guidelines Paul gives in 1 Corinthians 7 for dynamic sex?

2. What are the three kinds of sex I've described? What are the things a man needs to do to meet his wife's sexual needs?

3. How can you discover what your wife enjoys?

4. What can you do to strengthen the spiritual side of your marriage relationship?

5. For additional insights on the physical side of marriage, I recommend John Gray's book *Mars and Venus in the Bedroom*, published by HarperCollins.

The M Word

One of the most frequently asked questions I get from men isn't, "Do you believe in aliens?" "Do you think dogs go to heaven?" Or "How hot is it in hell?" Nobody ever asks me important questions like those.

What men want to know is my view on masturbation. More specifically, they want to know what the Bible says about the subject.

If you look up the word *masturbate* (or any of its synonyms) in *Young's Analytical Concordance to the Bible* you won't find a single reference. Know why? Because the Bible is silent on the subject.

It's important to remember that when God gave the Law he handed down some specific rules to identify sexual sins (Deuteronomy 22:13–30). He did this to protect his people and to provide for their needs in a healthy way.

Since God saw Jewish boys and men masturbating, I think it's significant that he chose not to condemn the behavior. I realize there are a few Christian writers who would disagree with me. Some try to prove masturbation is wrong by referring to the Old Testament character Onan. After the death of Onan's brother, he had a responsibility to produce offspring with his brother's widow, Tamar (Genesis 38:8–10; Deuteronomy 25:5–6). Apparently Onan wanted to have sex with Tamar but didn't want to father children. To keep her from getting pregnant, "whenever he lay with his brother's wife, he spilled his semen on the ground" (Genesis 38:9). Onan's behavior so displeased the Lord that he took Onan's life (Genesis 38:10).

Even a casual reading of this passage reveals that it has nothing to do with masturbation. God didn't condemn Onan for masturbating. In fact he was having intercourse. God punished him for using Tamar to satisfy his sexual desire without fulfilling his responsibility to his brother.

The Four-Part Masturbation Test

Since the Bible is silent on the subject how can a man know if it's wrong for him to masturbate? I think the best way to answer a question that the Bible doesn't specifically address is to see what it says about related subjects. Fortunately, the Bible is clear on the subject of sexual purity. I've examined the Scriptures and identified four tests aimed at helping a man determine whether or not his behavior is pure.

TEST ONE: **Your Thoughts**

In Matthew 5:28 (NIV) Jesus said, "Anyone who looks at a woman lustfully has already committed adultery with her in his heart." While the act of masturbation may be amoral, fantasizing about having sex with someone other than your wife is clearly wrong.

The words of Jesus would indicate that masturbation is wrong when accompanied by reading pornographic literature, viewing pornographic images, or thinking about past erotic images you've viewed.

By the way, I've searched the Bible for loopholes and there are none. If you fuel your lust with porn or memories of women besides your wife, it's wrong.

It's not that masturbating is wrong. Rather it's what you do with your thoughts and eyes that make it wrong. Can you masturbate and maintain pure thoughts? Or is that impossible for you? Only you know the answer to that question.

TEST TWO: Self-Control

Several years ago a young man told me he masturbated four or five times a day. His entire life revolved around when and where he would masturbate. While his case is an extreme example, there are other men who find they can't resist the urge to masturbate. In 1 Corinthians 6:12 (NIV), Paul wrote, " 'Everything is permissible for me' — but not everything is beneficial. 'Everything is permissible for me' — but I will not be mastered by anything." While masturbation may not be wrong, it is wrong for our lives to be controlled by habitual or compulsive masturbation. If you can't control your urge to masturbate then you're not being controlled by the new man God created within you. You're being controlled by your flesh.

TEST THREE: Love

As we saw in the last chapter Paul made it clear that a husband is to meet the sexual needs of his wife (1 Corinthians 7:3). A failure to do so is a sin and demonstrates a lack of love for her. When masturbation drains a man of the sexual energy needed to care for his wife it's wrong.

TEST FOUR: Your Conscience

Paul talked with the Romans about how they should view practices not condemned by God but by some believers. He said, "Blessed is the man who does not condemn himself by what he approves. But the man who has doubts is condemned if he eats, because his eating is not from faith; and everything that does not come from faith is sin" (Romans 14:22–23 NIV).

If you apply the first three tests to your practice of masturbation but your conscience bothers you then Paul would admonish you to stop the behavior. My guess would be that you've deceived yourself into believing your behavior doesn't violate one of the first three tests and that's why your conscience is condemning you.

Or it could be your conscience is overly sensitive and needs to be educated. If you feel guilty about behaviors that are not wrong, then you need to examine the source of your guilt.

When is it okay to masturbate?

There are as many unique situations as there are men. It would be impossible and foolish for me to try to walk though each one. I believe the four tests I've mentioned provide a guideline that could be applied to most situations.

Ask yourself:

1. "Does my behavior involve impure thoughts?"
2. "Am I in control of my behavior, or am I controlled by my lust?"
3. "Is my behavior preventing me from meeting my wife's sexual needs?"
4. "Is my conscience clear? Am I acting in faith?"

Each of us has to determine before God whether our attitudes and actions are pleasing to him. Ultimately, this is a decision you must make. I'm not going to try and out-god God by condemning a behavior he refused to address. If God considered it a sin he would have said so.

But let's suppose you know you can't masturbate without violating one or all of the rules above. How can you control yourself?

How to Control the Urge

The message of this book has been that your sexual behavior flows from your identity. When your flesh craves gratification that's fueled by lust then the behavior is not coming from the new man in you. It's coming from your sinful appetites. It's crucial you deal with the temptation as laid out in chapters 12–15. Read them again and put them into practice. The more you live in accordance with your new identity, the greater control you'll exercise over your mind, your eyes, and your sexual appetites.

My Opinion

Unless a guy is compulsively masturbating, denying his wife, or using porn to charge up his lust, I don't make a big deal out of masturbating. As I said earlier, telling a man not to masturbate is like telling a dog not to bark. Or maybe I said it's like telling a duck not to quack. Anyway, I see a lot of kids and men who seem overwhelmed with guilt because they masturbate. My advice is to pursue God, seek purity, and lighten up on this. Having read this paragraph — go back and read the first sentence again.

FOR DISCUSSION

1. Why do you think the Bible is silent on masturbation?

2. What are the four tests for purity that should govern a man's behavior?

3. When would it be okay for a man to masturbate?

4. Why is a man's identity important to a life of sexual purity?

5. What advice would you give to a man who asked you whether or not he should masturbate? Why?

For Wives Only

If you're a wife, and your husband is reading this book, or if you bought it for him, I'd like to offer you some encouragement. Since I don't know the specifics of your husband's situation, I'm going to address you as though he has, or needs to, talk with you about his desire to live a sexually pure life. It may be he's never committed a serious sexual sin and is taking preventative action. Or it could be he's gone way over the line. Whatever his circumstances, this little chapter is intended to help you support your husband. I realize this may be one of the shortest chapters you've ever read, but its seven points are crucial.

First, I'd urge you to read the rest of this book after you've looked over this chapter, if you haven't done so already. I believe that's important because it will help you better understand your husband and the battles he may face. It will also give you insights into your identity in Christ so you can live in a way that reflects the new you. As you read the book please remember that I wrote it for men, not women. A lot of the language I used and stories I told are intended to connect with guys. Don't let the man-talk prevent you from gleaning some insights from the book.

Second, you could be your husband's most important ally. I said "could be" because most couples seldom, if ever, discuss a husband's struggles with sexual lust. Just as they seldom discuss a woman's battles with compulsive eating (my surveys indicate 55 percent of the men questioned sometimes struggle with sexually compulsive behavior and 55 percent of the women sometimes battle with compulsive eating). The point is, men and women alike have areas of weakness that they prefer not to talk about.

That's the case because there's so much shame associated with secret sins that we want to keep them hidden as long as possible. Who wants to talk about something they're ashamed of?

So if the two of you discuss his struggle, you'll be in a position to provide him with much needed prayer and encouragement. While the process may be painful, the outcome could be a stronger marriage and a union that honors God.

> *I think it's significant for you to know*
> *that if you're talking about his battle for purity,*
> *that's a positive statement about your marriage.*

Third, if he's struggling with sexual purity, you need to know that his battle isn't about you. It's understandable for a woman to feel rejected when she discovers that her husband finds other women attractive. That feeling of rejection could be intensified if she discovers he has looked at porn on the Internet or done something worse.

It's important to know that all men struggle with sexual lust at one time or another, regardless of the beauty of their wife. In fact, some men battle to maintain purity even though they have a great marriage. As I noted in the first two chapters, men are wired to find women attractive. That's not a bad thing since God made us that way. But the downside is it's easy for a man's lust to grab hold of that natural attraction and use it to fuel sinful thoughts and actions.

Fourth, I would encourage you and your husband to talk openly with one another about his fight for purity. I make that statement with a bit of hesitation because I know there is the potential for great hurt and harm. Ideally, couples should be able to talk openly and honestly about everything.

So you may wonder what would keep your husband from talking with you — apart from the shame I mentioned above. While I don't know your husband personally, I can tell you most men fear that if they confess to their wife that they've visited a porn site on the Internet or stumbled in some other way, she'll respond with an emotional outburst. Sometimes the initial outburst will be followed by withdrawal. Afterward, he'll regret telling her.

With that in mind, it's crucial for you to do everything you can to rely on the Lord and not respond with an emotional outburst. I'm not suggesting you should not respond emotionally. You'd have to throw away your humanity to do that. Rather, I'm urging you to control how you express your emotions. You may be hurt ... as you should be. You could feel betrayed ... maybe you were. But pray for the grace you need to express those feelings in a way that will encourage him to keep talking with you.

If he's opening up with you, it's because he loves you and needs your support. If you respond with an emotional outburst, I can almost guarantee you he'll pull back and not address the subject with you again. Most men would rather live with a lie than an angry and emotional wife. I know this may sound harsh, and I don't mean it that way, but you need to decide which you want: the pain of honesty or the painlessness of a lie or ignorance.

Cindy and I decided a long time ago that we would prefer the pain of honesty. Why? Because the truth is something we can process and work with. A lie is like Jell-O — it may taste good to the mind, but it doesn't have the kind of substance you can do anything with.

> *Truth in a marriage is better*
> *than untruth or ignorance.*

Fifth, tell him how he has hurt you but affirm him for telling you the truth. If you feel disappointed and betrayed, tell him. But let him know you're glad he values openness enough to tell you. If he asks for your forgiveness, which he may do, forgive him. But let him know that you want to know what specific steps he's going to take to prevent this from happening again. Let him know it will take time for you to trust him again but that you're willing to get to that place.

Sixth, remember that it's not your job as a wife to fix your husband. That's God's job. Avoid the trap of continually checking up on him. God will work best in his life if you allow someone else to do that and you support him with your prayers. And don't ask for the specific details of his sin. The details won't help you and it won't help him to tell you.

Seventh, find someone who can help you process your emotions and support you as you encourage your husband. After you've talked with your husband, if you need to vent your emotions, pour them out to God. Talk with a pastor or trusted friend. It may be that the two of you will need to seek the help of a counselor as you work through this.

I'm thankful that my wife, Cindy, has always offered me her support. I once asked her why she never got upset when I confessed a bad decision on my part, and she said, "I didn't get upset because I knew you'd deal with it. I had confidence in your commitment to Christ and I trusted you."

Of course, you may not have that kind of confidence in your husband. And maybe what he's done was serious enough that you shouldn't trust him — at least not until he's proven that he's worthy of your trust. But it's still a good idea for you to hope for change and trust God to bring it about in his life as you support him with your prayers.

If this process proves confusing and painful and you feel you need additional insight and support, I'd encourage you to read one of the following books:

> *Living With Your Husband's Secret Wars* by Marsha Means
>
> *An Affair of the Mind* by Laurie Hall
>
> *When His Secret Sin Breaks Your Heart* by Kathy Gallagher

I think the words of these women will help heal your wounds and strengthen you so you can better support your husband.

Hopefully, as the two of you work through this challenge, your lines of communication will be more open and your marriage stronger. Hopefully your husband will live a life of purity that provides you with the love and security you need. During such challenging times it's important to remember that God delights in using our weakness as a vessel for his strength (2 Corinthians 12:9). As your husband experiences God's power in his place of weakness, his life will be a source or encouragement to others — and your willingness to be his ally could enable you to encourage other wives when they face a similar challenge.

FOR DISCUSSION

1. Why is it important for husbands and wives to discuss their spiritual struggles with one another?

2. What are the two reasons that cause men to avoid talking openly with their wives about their struggle with sexual purity?

3. How should a man approach his wife if he's going to talk with her about this? How should he respond if she's hurt?

4. What may a man have to give up to restore his wife's trust? Why is this important?

5. What kind of a plan should a man have before talking with his wife? Do you have such a plan? If so, what is it?

21

Tools for Tight Corners

I used to have a neighbor, Ernie Bellone, who bought tools he never used. A box would arrive with a tool he had purchased, and he wouldn't even open it. He'd just stack it on top of the other boxes in the back of his garage.

One day I asked him about his extravagant practice, and he said, "I want the tool just in case I need it."

I'm not a handyman, and unlike Ernie, I don't collect tools. I can, however, disassemble anything and put it back together again. Unfortunately, there are always parts left over, and the thing doesn't work. In light of my bumbling repair skills it surprised my wife when I said I'd take out the old kitchen faucet and put in a new one.

"You sure you want to do this?" she asked. "Seems like the last time you tried to repair something it ended up costing a lot of money."

Her words made me feel small; so I stood up tall and said, "I'm smarter than a faucet." And just to drive home how positive I felt about the upcoming job, I said, "It's not like I'm doing something complicated like pulling up an edge of the carpet so I can run a stereo wire under it." That was the last job I'd bumbled.

Anyway, I rummaged through an old cardboard box where I had tossed some greasy tools. I found a socket wrench and snapped a fitting on the end. As I crawled under the sink, Cindy asked, "How long will this take?"

From inside the cabinet I said, "Thirty minutes. Definitely thirty minutes. No longer."

An hour later she returned and asked if I had finished the first job and was working on another. I never thought sarcasm became her.

Actually, I would have finished in thirty minutes except for a single problem: my wrench wouldn't fit through the tiny space between the back of the sink and the wall. I tried every conceivable angle, but I couldn't get the end of the wrench over the head of the nut. I did, however, manage to mangle the knuckles of my right hand.

Just as I was about to give up and concede to Cindy I would need to call a plumber, I remembered Ernie. A couple of minutes later I found my friend in his garage.

I explained my problem and Ernie thought for a moment. Then a circuit connected in his brain, his face lit up, and he said, "I have a set of plumber's tools made exactly for that job." He then pulled an unopened box from the top of another box on a shelf in his garage and handed it to me. "It's a set of wrench extensions. You'll be the first to use them."

His smile said, "I'm smarter than you because I buy tools before I need them."

My smile said, "I'll pretend you're really smart because if I don't, you'll take back your tool."

Five minutes later I had the first nut off as Ernie stood over me. Suddenly an impossible job became a breeze, and I felt like a master plumber ... a skilled handyman ... a prize of a husband. All because I had a tool designed and built to get around a tight corner. My joy was so great that Cindy didn't even try to squelch it with a reminder of how long it had taken me.

Tools That Come In Handy

As you move forward with your life of sexual purity, you'll occasionally find yourself in a tight corner. Try as you might, you won't be able to work your way out of it. Temptation, disappointment, or relapse will cause you to fear you're not going to make it. At such times — you'll feel like giving up.

> *The good news is*
> *you've got some tools in a box*
> *that will be here*
> *when you need them.*

You may not need all those tools now, but when you're in a tight corner, you'll be glad they're here. Read this chapter carefully so you'll know where each tool is located. Mark those tools you may need first, so you'll be able to find them quickly.

Telling Your Wife

Men often ask me if they should tell their wife about their struggle with sexual lust. Ideally, a man should be able to discuss everything with his wife. Honesty strengthens relationships and dishonesty weakens them. Obviously, some sins are more serious than others, and you need to exercise wisdom as you broach the subject.

I'd suggest you allow her to read this book before you talk with her. As you probably noticed, the previous chapter was written for her. If she reads the entire book she'll better understand where you're coming from. It will also increase the likelihood she'll come alongside you as an ally, and it will convince her you're serious about your pursuit of purity.

If you talk with your wife I'd encourage you to assure her of your love and commitment. Be prepared for her to respond emotionally because she'll likely feel betrayed and threatened. You'll have to absorb that without withdrawing or covering your tracks to appease her anger.

It will help her if you've got a specific plan for purity. She'll feel more secure if she knows you're taking aggressive steps to protect yourself from temptation. To restore her trust it's likely that you'll have to forfeit some of your freedom for awhile. By that I mean she may want to know where you're going and how long you intend to be there. She may want a better idea of where you spend your money. I'd urge you to go along with her need for more information about how you spend your time.

If you need to seek her forgiveness, be sure and read the tool for seeking forgiveness below. Hopefully, as you move forward toward purity, your marriage will emerge stronger than ever.

A Safety Guard against Rituals

A good power saw has a safety guard to protect your hands and allow you to cut wood without cutting off a finger. In overcoming compulsive sexual behavior, you need safety guards in place. It's crucial for you to identify the circumstances, conversations, and relationships that prompt you to act out. All trigger objects or events must have a safety guard around them.

You can construct such a shield by identifying the rituals that trigger your compulsive and sinful behavior and removing them from your life. Get a sheet of paper and use the following format to build a guard over your rituals.

Rituals

1. _____
2. _____
3. _____
4. _____
5. _____
6. _____
7. _____

How I'll Avoid Them

1. _____
2. _____
3. _____
4. _____
5. _____
6. _____
7. _____

Patient Hope

Don't be surprised if after a few days or weeks of abstinence, your lust comes roaring out of its cave. Sexual lust is deep-rooted and takes time to overcome. The words of Isaiah offer encouragement: "Those who hope in the LORD will renew their strength. They will soar on wings like eagles; they will run and not grow weary, they will walk and not be faint" (Isaiah 40:31 NIV).

Pain

As you grow in your freedom from sexual lust, it's important to remember that pain isn't your enemy. Pain is a tool that will make you stronger. Don't run away from it or try to deaden it with sexual sins.

Eventually that which deadens pain creates more suffering than it eliminated.

Instead of running from the pain, ride it out as you would a rising tide. Eventually your lustful cravings will recede as your new man asserts control over you.

Nobody passes through life without hardship. Even the apostle Paul experienced intense pain caused by a "thorn in my flesh" (2 Corinthians 12:7–9). While we don't know the source of his pain, we know he suffered greatly. Three times he begged God to take it away. Three times God refused. Instead of removing the cause of his suffering, God gave Paul an extra measure of his grace.

Rather than becoming angry with God, Paul wrote, "I will boast all the more gladly about my weaknesses, so that Christ's power may rest on me. That is why, for Christ's sake, I delight in weaknesses, in insults, in hardships, in persecutions, in difficulties. For when I am weak, then I am strong" (2 Corinthians 12:9–10 NIV).

Paul learned how to rely on the grace of God during times of suffering. While the pain wasn't removed, he experienced the strength needed to endure it with dignity.

Thankfully, that same grace is available to you. When you hurt, ask God to give you the grace needed to endure. Ask him to make his strength apparent through your weakness.

It's important to know that the place of greatest pain will also be the place of God's greatest work in your life — and it will also be God's greatest work through your life. As others see God carry you through hardship, they'll want to give him a try. God's provision at your point of weakness and pain is his preparation for your future ministry.

Remember, this book resulted from God helping me in my battle with lust.

A Consequence and Benefits List

Usually the pleasure of acting out is limited to a few minutes or hours, but the consequences may last a lifetime. Many men who were once addicted have found that comparing the consequences of acting out with the benefits of abstinence helps them avoid acting out. Periodically turn to chapter 10, beginning on page 125, and complete or review the exercises outlined there under the heading "Make a List."

Tears

Crying isn't something men do publicly. Some men don't even cry in private. Yet tears are tools that help us heal. I once read that tears are the body's way of washing away toxic chemicals. Tears cleanse the body and soul. When we hold them back, we dam up an emotional stream that needs to flow for the heart to stay pure.

Even Jesus cried. When his friends Martha and Mary wept over the death of their brother, Lazarus, Jesus also wept (John 11:35). His rough carpenter's hands wiped the tears from his cheeks.

As you review the hurt you've suffered, you may need to cry. Disappointment may have taken a toll. Go ahead and weep. It's okay. Grieve over your disappointments and losses. God understands. As you cry, imagine Jesus wrapping his strong arms around you. God loves you and desires to heal your hurts.

Forgiveness

Forgiveness is a priceless tool for finding healing and freedom from your lust. There are three dimensions of forgiveness you need to employ.

Dimension One: Finding forgiveness. No matter what you've done, God offers you forgiveness. Regardless of how terrible your shame and torturous your guilt, forgiveness is yours for the taking.

There is no need for you to continue to punish yourself for past wrongs. Jesus died on the cross and was punished in your place. He took upon himself all of your wrongdoing and suffered the punishment you deserved (2 Corinthians 5:21; Romans 5:8). Three days later he rose from the dead, leaving your guilt and shame forever buried.

His forgiveness is available. Simply express to him your desire to accept him and his forgiveness (John 3:16). Once you've been forgiven by God, there's no need to condemn yourself. When you hear voices of self-condemnation, say to yourself, "God forgives me and I forgive myself."

Dimension Two: Extending Forgiveness. As God has forgiven you, so you must forgive those who hurt you. That's not easy, especially if your wounds are deep and festering. But healing requires cleaning them out by forgiving those who hurt you.

"But I can't forgive them," you might say. "You don't understand what they've done to me."

You're right, I don't. I'm sorry you've been hurt. But you've certainly not been brutalized more than Jesus was when the Romans nailed him to the cross. Yet God's Son extended forgiveness to those who killed him (Luke 23:34).

"But I'm not God's Son," you may argue.

I realize that. But if you'll turn to God, his Son will give you the strength you need to forgive. Remember, you are a new man — a good man in Christ. When you forgive, you're acting from your new identity, not your old one.

But you need to be aware that there's a difference between forgiveness and reconciliation. Reconciliation can occur only when the offending person realizes the depth of hurt they've caused and seeks forgiveness. You may forgive a wrong but if the person who wronged you minimizes what they've done, it's unlikely you'll be reconciled. Yet even when reconciliation *doesn't* occur, you still need to forgive.

Once you've told God you forgive the one who hurt you, each time you remember the hurt, instead of reviewing the wrong, pray for them. Prayer is a great antidote for bitterness and wrath. In fact, I don't believe it's possible to harbor bitterness against someone you're consistently praying for.

Dimension Three: Seeking Forgiveness. It may be you've hurt others while acting out sexually. As you reflect on your past, people you've hurt may come to mind. You may need to seek forgiveness from those people.

Before you get in touch with them, think through what you'll say. Avoid blaming them for your actions. Nobody wants to hear someone who's hurt them say something like,

"After you lied and cheated me out of my money, I became angry and said some unkind words. Will you forgive me?"

Be honest and straight to the point. When I go to those I've hurt, I say something like this: "I now see that I've wronged you by [my offense]. I'm deeply sorry. Will you forgive me?" I suggest you use a similar approach.

I encourage people to make these contacts in person or over the phone. Writing out your request for forgiveness in an email or letter isn't a good idea unless it's the only way to communicate with the person. A letter or email could fall into the wrong hands and cause greater pain.

Wounded people are sometimes suspicious of attempts at reconciliation. They may even withhold forgiveness. Don't argue with them or try to persuade them. Tell them you understand, and request their prayers. If they pray for you, the time may come when they'll forgive you.

It's important to realize that people who forgive you aren't obligated to renew the friendship. You're not seeking total restoration of the relationship. You're simply seeking forgiveness. If something more occurs, that's great. But be careful not to place undue expectations on the other person.

Also, be sure to weigh the benefits of seeking forgiveness from a person you've wronged against the harm you could cause that person by approaching him or her about the offense. Sometimes the most loving thing to do is accept God's forgiveness and leave it at that.

Bible Meditation

Nothing helps me maintain sexual purity like memorizing and meditating on Bible verses that address my needs. Just as sin seeks to define you, meditation on Scripture nurtures the new you in Christ, the real you.

The following passages have proven helpful to me. Whenever I'm discouraged or tempted, I review them and gain direction and strength.

Temptation

No temptation has seized you except what is common to man. And God is faithful; he will not let you be tempted beyond what you can bear. But when you are tempted, he will also provide a way out so that you can stand up under it (1 Corinthians 10:13 NIV).

Blessed is the man who perseveres under trial, because when he has stood the test, he will receive the crown of life that God has promised to those who love him. When tempted, no one should say, "God is tempting me." For God cannot be tempted by evil, nor does he tempt anyone; but each one is tempted when, by his own evil desire, he is dragged away and enticed. Then, after desire has conceived, it gives birth to sin; and sin, when it is full-grown, gives birth to death (James 1:12–15 NIV).

Anxiety

Do not be anxious about anything, but in everything, by prayer and petition, with thanksgiving, present your requests to God. And the peace of God, which transcends all understanding, will guard your hearts and your minds in Christ Jesus (Philippians 4:6–7 NIV).

Pure Thoughts

Finally, brothers, whatever is true, whatever is noble, whatever is right, whatever is pure, whatever is lovely, whatever is admirable — if anything is excellent or praiseworthy — think about such things (Philippians 4:8 NIV).

Lust

Flee from sexual immorality. All other sins a man commits are outside his body, but he who sins sexually sins against his own body (1 Corinthians 6:18 NIV).

Contentment

Keep your lives free from the love of money and be content with what you have, because God has said, "Never will I leave you; never will I forsake you" (Hebrews 13:5 NIV).

Forgiveness

Peter came to Jesus and asked, "Lord, how many times shall I forgive my brother when he sins against me? Up to seven times?" Jesus answered, "I tell you, not seven times, but seventy-seven times" (Matthew 18:21–22 NIV).

If we confess our sins, he is faithful and just and will forgive us our sins and purify us from all unrighteousness (1 John 1:9 NIV).

Blessed is he whose transgressions are forgiven, whose sins are covered (Psalm 32:1 NIV).

Prayer

The LORD is near to all who call on him, to all who call on him in truth (Psalm 145:18 NIV).

Ask and it will be given to you; seek and you will find; knock and the door will be opened to you. For everyone who asks receives; he who seeks finds; and to him who knocks, the door will be opened (Matthew 7:7–8 NIV).

Your New Man

> Therefore, if anyone is in Christ, he is a new creation; the old has gone, the new has come! (2 Corinthians 5:17 NIV).

> I have been crucified with Christ and I no longer live, but Christ lives in me. The life I live in the body, I live by faith in the Son of God, who loved me and gave himself for me (Galatians 2:20 NIV).

> Since, then, you have been raised with Christ, set your hearts on things above, where Christ is seated at the right hand of God. Set your minds on things above, not on earthly things. For you died, and your life is now hidden with Christ in God (Colossians 3:1–3 NIV).

Prayer

Prayer is talking with God. It's the way you stay connected with the one who gives you his love and acceptance along with the power needed to live as a new man.

If prayer isn't something you've ever scheduled, I encourage you to pray while you drive. Turn off your radio and carry on a conversation with God. Do it aloud. Once you develop the habit, try to carve out a time slot each day when you can get alone with God and pray.

Remember, the object of your lust gives you an illusion of intimacy. Only authentic intimacy with God will expose the illusion. Jesus made it clear that we remain in him through prayer and Bible meditation (John 15:7). God wants you to enjoy him so your need for the illusion of intimacy isn't there. View your times of prayer and Bible reading as opportunities to draw near to God.

Journaling

I regularly try to write in my journal. That doesn't mean I write pages of poetry. It involves recording the key events of the day and noting my spiritual temperature. I also try to write out a prayer or two so I'll have something to refer back to when my prayers are answered.

Keeping a journal is a tangible way of strengthening your new man. Remember, sin seeks to steal your identity and weaken the new man within you. Bible meditation, prayer, and journaling strengthen your spirit by deepening your friendship with God and nurturing your new man.

Rebound

It's crucial for you to have a relapse strategy. It would be great if you'd never stumble again, but you may. If you do, get back up.

You may tend to think, "Now that I've blown it, I might as well quit trying." Where do you think that comes from? Your sin or the new man in you? Avoid such stupid and destructive thinking. If you relapse, rebound. You're not starting over. Focus on the fact that you went for a while without acting out sinfully. Allow your disappointment to be a reminder of your vulnerability and need to depend on God and avoid certain situations.

God has forgiven you. Accept his forgiveness and move on.

FOR DISCUSSION

1. Skim back through this chapter and mark the tools you think you'll need in the future. Why did you pick the ones you marked?

2. Pick a Scripture verse that helps you the most and meditate on it for a week, asking God to help you experience the reality it represents. Try to memorize the passage. Share it with your group.

3. Which of the ideas in this chapter will you implement first? Why?

4. What's the most important thing you gleaned from this book? How does it compare with what you said you hoped to get out of the book at the end of chapter 1?

A Final
(Very Short) Story

I wish the two of us could talk personally. Maybe one day we will.

But before we part, I want to remind you that a life of purity flows from your true identity as a son of God. As you grow in your understanding of that single reality, your thoughts and actions will be transformed. Slowly you'll find yourself acting in a way that's consistent with the new man, the good man, that God has made you.

I'm reminded of the story of a college student who carried around ten extra pounds, never played a sport, and enjoyed eating more than competing against other guys. He never thought of himself as athletic and never aspired to play sports.

One day, as he walked across campus, the track coach approached him and asked, "What's your name?"

"Jeremiah Johnson."

"Anybody ever tell you that you're a runner?"

"No. Never."

"Well, it's true," the coach said. "I can tell by the way you walk. How about letting me clock you this afternoon?"

"I don't think so," Jeremiah said.

Unwilling to take no for an answer the coach persisted until Jeremiah agreed to show up for track practice. As he entered the locker room after school he felt as out of place as a mule at a horse race. Chiding himself for agreeing to the coach's request, he slipped on some shorts and running shoes and walked outside to the track. After stretching and jogging a few laps, the coached called him over.

As a few of the other sprinters watched, Jeremiah surprised himself, and everyone else, except the coach, by running some impressive times. The coach called him aside and said, "Hey, what did I tell you, Jeremiah? If you'll let me work with you I think you could become one of the best runners in the country."

"The country?" Jeremiah asked.

"You heard me," the coach said. "You've got the stride and quick twitch muscles that nobody can coach. You just need to get in shape and learn how to leave the blocks."

Over the next year Jeremiah worked hard. In fact, he worked harder than he had ever worked at anything in his life. And it paid off because he won the conference championship in the 100 meters.

A week before the national meet he was at a fraternity party when the best-looking girl in the house approached him and offered Jeremiah a plate of Doritos and a cold beer. "This is for you," she said.

In that moment he had to make a quick decision — and the decision would be based on how he viewed himself. If he saw himself as a bundle of nerves and unsatisfied appetites he'd take the beer and hope he'd get the girl too. But he didn't see himself that way, and so he looked at the girl, smiled, and turned down her offer.

"Why? Don't you believe in drinking?" she asked.

"Oh, that's not why I'm saying no."

"Then what's the reason?"

"I'm a runner," he said.[1]

When a man sees himself as a runner, it's easy to turn down a plate of Doritos and a cold beer. Why? Because runners don't eat or drink anything that will slow them down. It's just not who they are.

Similarly, the more you see yourself as a son of God, a new man, a good man, a man indwelt by God's Spirit, the more you'll think and act like a new creation. The less you'll find yourself attracted to attitudes and actions that are inconsistent with your new identity. But as a good man, you'll still be tempted. And now you know how to handle temptation in a way that will bring victory — one temptation at a time. If you stumble, you know how to get back up again, with the help of a friend, and move forward as a son of God.

I don't know about you, but I'm excited about the work God is going to do in and through you as you grasp your new identity.

By the way, the apple on the cover isn't the fruit Adam was tempted with in the Garden. It's an image of the new man, the good man, that God has made you — the golden delicious apple tree.

Notes

Chapter 1: Why Naked Dogs Look So Dressed

1. *Brain Basics: Understanding Sleep.* This was an article from the website: National Institute of Neurological Disorders and Strokes (NIH Publication No. 06–3440-c).
2. Tim Allen, *Don't Stand Too Close to a Naked Man* (New York: Hyperion, 1994), 53–54.

Chapter 2: Why Naked Women Look So Good

1. Mike Mason, *The Mystery of Marriage* (Portland: Multnomah, 1985), 115.
2. Ibid., 114.
3. S. Craig Glickman, *A Song for Lovers* (Downers Grove, Ill.: InterVarsity, 1976), 21.
4. Ibid., 24–25.

Chapter 3: Why Other Women Look Better

1. Judson Poling and Bill Perkins, *The Journey* (Grand Rapids, Mich.: Zondervan, 1996), 3.

Chapter 5: The Thrill of Young Love

1. H. Eist and A. Mandel, "Family Treatment of On-going Incest Behavior," *Family Process* (1967), 7:216.

Chapter 6: How Big Is Your Problem?

1. Patrick Carnes, *Out of the Shadows* (Minneapolis: CompCare, 1983), 160.
2. Ibid., 27.
3. Craig Nakken, *The Addictive Personality* (New York: Harper & Row, 1988), 24.

Chapter 7: Three Ways to Lose the Battle

1. Eugene H. Peterson, *The Message* (Colorado Springs: NavPress, 1993, 1994, 1995), 375.

Chapter 8: Crawl Into the Cave and Drag Out the Bear

1. John Bradshaw, *Healing the Shame That Binds You* (Deerfield Beach, Fla.: HCI; 2005), 12–13.

Chapter 9: Grab the Grace of God

1. "Mystery of Exploding Toads," BBC News (April 27, 2005).
2. M. Scott Peck, *People of the Lie* (New York: Simon & Schuster), 76.
3. Ibid., 76.

Chapter 10: Count the Cost

1. *The American Heritage Dictionary of the English Language*, 4th edition (New York: Houghton Mifflin, 2006).
2. Abraham Twerski, *Addictive Thinking* (San Francisco: Harper & Row, 1990), 79–80.
3. Jay Dennis, *Taming Your Private Thoughts* (Grand Rapids, Mich.: Zondervan, 2002), 17–18.

Chapter 13: Four Steps to Freedom

1. David Needham, *Birthright* (Sisters, Ore.: Multnomah, 999), 82–84.

Chapter 14: Guard Your Thoughts

1. *Family Safe Media*.
2. From a *Christianity Today* survey (2000).
3. From a *Focus on the Family* poll (October 1, 2003).

Chapter 16: The Four Phases of Friendship

1. Allen, *Don't Stand Too Close*, 84.
2. Ibid., 86–87.
3. Herb Goldberg, *The Hazards of Being Male* (New York: New American Library, 1976), 133.
4. Ibid., 136–37.

Chapter 17: What to Look for in a Friend

1. Rod Cooper also tells part of this story in his book *Double Bind*, (Grand Rapids, Mich.: Zondervan, 1996), 19–20.

Chapter 18: For Married Men Only

1. John Gray, *Mars and Venus in the Bedroom* (New York: HarperCollins, 1995), 86.

Chapter 22: A Final (Very Short) Story

1. I'm thankful to David Needham for this great illustration, which I've altered a bit. It's taken from pages 91–92 of his book *Birthright*, noted previously.

Acknowledgments

I'd like to thank my band of brothers. Over the years you've coached, corrected, comforted, and challenged me. I thank God for your friendship. I hate to think who I'd be without you. Bob Bobosky, Dave Carr, Rod Cooper, Lane Kagey, and Bob Noack.

Thanks to everyone at Zondervan for their belief in this book and to Bob Hudson who edited the revision. Thanks, Bob, for helping smooth out the rough places.

Awaken the Leader Within

How the Wisdom of Jesus Can Unleash Your Potential

Bill Perkins

Vision and motivation to become the leader God intends you to be—whether you're leading your family, church, coworkers, or a Fortune 500 company.

You're a leader! In fact, every time you try to get someone to do something you want done, you're exercising leadership. This book will help you discover from Jesus how to lead more effectively as you understand the character traits and practical skills of a true leader. A discussion guide in the back of the book will help you integrate the principles into your life as you allow Jesus to help you learn how to cultivate and cast a vision, make wise decisions, build a team, harness opposing forces, facilitate innovation, and put others first.

Softcover 0-310-24291-6

Pick up a copy today at your favorite bookstore!

We want to hear from you. Please send your comments about this book to us in care of zreview@zondervan.com. Thank you.

ZONDERVAN.com/
AUTHORTRACKER
follow your favorite authors

For more information about Million Mighty Men
or to contact Bill Perkins about speaking,
go to www.billperkins.com.

When Young Men Are Tempted

Sexual Purity for Guys in the Real World

Bill Perkins and Randy Southern

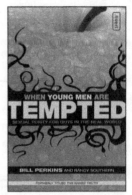

This practical look at sexual purity is written directly to teens in a frank, accessible, and totally honest style to help them make decisions for sexual integrity. *When Young Men Are Tempted* discusses factors surrounding sexual temptation and presents a strategy to encourage and assist young men to lead morally pure lives. Author Bill Perkins offers success stories as well as testimonies of false solutions. Readers will:

- Understand why "wrong" things seem so "right" and how sexual appetites get out of control
- Learn to filter and deal with the elements of teens' pop culture work
- Find freedom to confront and defeat the demons of sexual compromise, bad habits, and feelings of guilt—breaking addictive cycles
- User-friendly ways to make healthy decisions and act on them
- Discover strategies for ongoing victory

Upside-down. Turned around. Sound like a typical day for you? invert books meet you where you are—in the twisted, flipped around places in your life. You've got so many relationships to focus on—God, others, and even yourself—invert books will help you figure out how to give yourself fully to all of them. invert tackles the difficult topics that are important to you—and will help you turn to focus on God more clearly.

Softcover 0-310-27715-9